The
Hidden
Cleantech
Revolution

The Hidden Cleantech Revolution

Five Priorities for
Securing America's Energy Future
Without Breaking the Bank

John A. Moore
Chairman and CEO of Acorn Energy

and

Toby Shute
*Writer and Research Analyst
at* The Motley Fool

Energy Publishers of America
Houston • New York

To my wife, Beth, and my children, Haley, Henry,
Charlotte and Trixie.
Without you I am lost.
—John Moore

For my wonderful parents, Jackie and Bill,
and my incredible wife Ranee.
—Toby Shute

ISBN 978-0-615-39992-8

Cover design by Graham Roberts
Interior book design by Howard Roberts, HRoberts Design, Inc.

"In dreams begins responsibility."
— *William Butler Yeats*

CONTENTS

FOREWORD
Rethinking Opportunities
in Cleantech

The time is right for this book on Cleantech. During the past decade, an extraordinary number of events and circumstances have put energy-related issues more than ever front and center in our public debates, business decisions, and consumptive behaviors. While Hurricanes Katrina and Rita ravaged the Gulf coast, the climate change debate gained momentum and personal opinions on global warming impacted voting behavior in political races. Whereas sport-utility vehicles were hot commodities at the turn of the millennium, dramatic changes in taste left the United States auto industry in the hands of the government. The world has been witnessing extreme volatility in energy prices.

Amid this high degree of uncertainty on both the demand and supply sides, the issue of securing the energy infrastructure looms large. When will the first rolling brownouts or blackouts occur? Are the right investments being made to maintain our aged electrical grid? What if a terrorist attack on an important oil terminal succeeds, such as the one on the world's largest oil-processing facility in eastern Saudi Arabia in February 2006? What happens if the major trunk carriers for refined product went dry due to a prolonged flooding of the refinery infrastructure on the Gulf Coast?

It is no wonder that the stakes in energy are higher than ever before with uncertainty abounding and vast amounts of primary resources being imported into the United States. So stop for a moment and consider: What will help us transition through the *current* situation into a more secure energy future?

In this context, John Moore and Toby Shute have written a book to which we all ought to pay attention. The authors bring us back to energy basics while showing the way to the future: Our energy infrastructure is so vast that it takes many decades to transition the energy system away from the current dominance of fossil fuels. Equally important, this slow transition will be powered by those same fuels. Therefore, the only realistic proposition for having a *real impact now* in securing both energy and the environment is to further increase energy productivity by utilizing Cleantech in the systems we already have. The authors also imply that this solution requires significantly less resources than trying to rebuild our existing infrastructure with renewable energy. It's a powerful application of the 80–20 rule or Pareto principle I first learned to appreciate while working at The Boston Consulting Group.

John Moore is an experienced energy executive and a seasoned investor who lives by the insights he shares in this book. Both as an author and entrepreneur he blends industry knowledge and financial acumen with charisma and a real passion for our energy future. He puts his money where his words are. Securing our energy future by getting more out of what we've got is his insightful mantra. It is not just about cutting consumption. It is not just about efficiency gains. It is about energy productivity and how innovation in information technology delivers scalable Cleantech solutions for the energy sector *today*. Throughout the book, John Moore and Toby Shute, draw upon examples of companies and clean technologies that have reached practical solutions to fundamental energy problems in resource recovery, energy conversion and distribution, as well as energy security. Intelligence, as embedded in hardware and software, lies at the core of these solutions.

And business intelligence is what the authors bring to the reader. Toby Shute, who has been covering the energy industry for many years, imports the style of an intelligence briefing into the book similar to the type of briefing Fortune 500 CEOs or government officials receive. The book is easy to scan. And, it provides insight and, more importantly, foresight—allowing the reader to be proactive and anticipate the outcome of the hidden Cleantech revolution in the energy sector. The authors uncover activities and trends that are helping the energy industry to better meet society's needs and to increase its own productivity. Therefore, there is ample information about devices and software to be used by utilities, oil and gas companies, and other energy players. However, the reader will find little information on gadgets and "killer apps"—something like a super-battery, which, as the authors point out, is easily one of the most overhyped areas of Cleantech. "Killer apps" in Cleantech still need to prove that they can meet the 80-20 rule.

The book helps guide the investment professional to rethink opportunities in Cleantech, connecting the dots for specialists in the often disjointed energy industry sectors, and refocusing our attention from the ideological to the practical and innovative. It behooves us to fundamentally rethink the way we approach our energy future. This book does not dream about reinventing the world but shows the way to innovations that help to *reduce cost in supplying energy both financially and environmentally*. There is indeed a hidden Cleantech revolution. It is here, it is now, and it is real.

From my own observation and experience I couldn't agree more with the authors. During this economic recession energy-related research is still good business. So is the commercialization of energy technologies. And although I find it harder in the current environment to raise capital from investors for technology start-up companies, I still find sufficient strategic investors and industry partners to close both license and equity deals in

Cleantech as long as theses technologies have an impact on the existing energy system.

I can't emphasize enough the importance of the chapter that addresses the issue of impeded progress in coal-power generation fleet efficiency in the United States. New coal-fired units offer significant reductions in both coal usage and emissions. I don't know how people expect that wind and solar would be able to completely replace coal in the foreseeable future with lack of viable storage for intermittent power. Coal power plants are important base-load providers that enable and subsidize the transition to more renewables. So why not improve fleet efficiency and reduce emissions? It has worked in the past and it is happening in many countries around the world. Our clients at the Energy & Environmental Research Center are investing significant sums in cleaning up coal combustion. Many of these companies come to us from overseas, including China, looking for new concepts to reduce emissions and improve efficiencies. Opportunities abound.

I also appreciate John Moore and Toby Shute's attention to getting more out of oil and gas. After all, these two highly intertwined sectors account for over 60 percent of primary energy consumption in the United States. Looking at the current situation form a North Dakota perspective stresses the importance of the authors' proposition. First of all, oil production "peaked" in North Dakota in the mid-1980s and declined until 2003. Since then oil production has quadrupled or doubled over its highest production level in 1986 to about 300,000 barrels per day and continues to rapidly increase, making North Dakota the No. 4 onshore oil-producing state. A lot of this production comes from new Bakken wells employing horizontal drilling technology; oil that was considered previously not technically recoverable. In addition, North Dakota exports anthropogenic carbon dioxide for enhanced oil recovery into the Weyburn field in Canada in order to boost oil production. Overall, it is anticipated that some

20 million tons of carbon dioxide will be permanently seques-
tered over the lifespan of the project. The gas is being supplied
via a 205 mile long pipeline from the lignite-fired Dakota Gasification Company synfuels plant. The carbon dioxide project adds
about $30 million of gross revenue to the gasification plant's
cash flow each year. During its life, the Weyburn project is expected to produce at least 122 million barrels of incremental oil,
through displacement with carbon dioxide. From my experience
at the Energy & Environmental Research Center, which has been
involved in all of the above mentioned activities at some stage,
getting more out of what we've got does not only make sense
but also secures our energy future, environment, and economy.
North Dakota now has a very healthy state surplus indeed.

Lastly, I comment on the authors' almost obvious statement
that silicon scales better than steel. I say "almost obvious" as
many in the industry who should know better have gotten it
backwards. Clearly, the statement that there is an ongoing information revolution in the energy sector does not sound too revolutionary anymore after so many information revolutions before
in other sectors. However, what is most astounding is that many
Silicon Valley investors, who earned their money scaling silicon
in the past, when it came time for them recently to invest in the
clean energy sector they tried to scale steel instead and failed
miserably.

One final note before you read this book: Over the course
of new technology developments, many risks are taken. However, the closer one looks at the market realities these risks start
to become manageable. Suddenly, there appear real win-win
situations between technology developers and users that reduce
these risks and turn them into profits without prolonged government subsidies. Technology is more about integration of existing
components to deliver new solutions than creating new gadgets.
It is hard to overcome the inertia of the energy sector—unless
one can leverage it. John Moore and Toby Shute take you on a

journey that expands your horizon in Cleantech and should whet your appetite for more. The authors incite readers to think differently about energy and much beyond energy efficiency. They offer a powerful and cost-effective demonstration of what is being done in energy productivity for achieving a sustainable energy future.

Carsten Heide

Associate Director, Technology Commercialization and Intellectual Property Management, Energy & Environmental Research Center

INTRODUCTION
Making Energy Better

Modern societies require affordable and plentiful energy. Where energy supplies are unreliable, such as in much of Africa and the Middle East, economic development slows. Where they are stable, such as in the United States, Europe, Brazil and Taiwan, standards of living improve. It's no coincidence that China, the world's fastest-growing big economy, opens a new power plant every week. Coal is so central to the economic development of China that they refer to it as "country blood."

In the West we have long taken energy for granted. Most of us think about electricity only on those rare—though increasingly frequent—occasions when the lights go out. And 55 percent of Americans were not even alive to experience the Arab oil embargo of 1973.[1] For them, gas station lines remain an abstraction.

But times are changing. In the past few years, a number of factors (fuel price spikes, the Iraq War, the BP Gulf oil spill and prominent global warming summits, to name a few) have led consumers, businesspeople and citizens to devote greater attention to our energy future. From the White House to the coffee shop, the debate often simmers and sometimes rages. Do we cut consumption or increase production to advance our economic and environmental goals? Should we shift most transportation from one fuel to another? Is energy independence a reasonable expectation or a pipedream?

This national discussion is well meaning but too often misinformed. For example, there's a great deal of talk these days about solar and wind power, strategies that are destined to have negligible impact on our energy challenges for at least two *decades*. Yet existing technologies that can make the electric grid more efficient and reliable within the next two *years* sit gathering dust.

Why is this so? Partly because our energy infrastructure is vast, multifaceted and, to some extent, Balkanized; partly because those who go to work for oil and gas companies, utilities, and coal miners are engineering types who usually prefer doing to talking. They're in the game, but others are setting the rules.

We can't afford to go on this way.

Humanity stands today at an inflection point. For example, Americans dream of energy independence. With this goal in mind, can we ignore the fact that wind turbines and hybrid cars require rare earth minerals, a market that is 95 percent controlled by China?[2] Meanwhile, a worldwide consensus is forming (like it or not) around the idea that we must reduce carbon dioxide output, with wind energy touted among the answers. Are we to invest billions in this form of power without a single study that proves it will reduce our carbon output?

And another inconvenient truth confronts us: Simply maintaining our electrical grid at its current capacity will soon require a $1 trillion capital investment. The coal-fired plants that supply 50 percent of our electricity, for instance, on average have a 40-year life expectancy. At this writing, 70 percent of them are over 30 years old.[3]

Even if we set aside the enormous sums of money involved, these are not trivial concerns. Choices we make in the next ten years may determine the prosperity and security of our nation for the next hundred.

These commitments are too important to be decided without significant input from those who understand our current energy infrastructure best. And they are too important to be imposed upon one facet of the energy economy without considering the impact on all other facets.

With this book, the authors hope to bridge communications

gaps among players in the energy field and to give voice to those great operators and innovators whose voices are not being heard loudly enough in this most important debate. In it we'll survey across disciplines, analyzing and rating those technologies with the best chance for transforming our collective energy future not over the next hundred years, but in the next ten.

There are so many moving parts to the energy infrastructure that just deciding how to weigh one idea against another becomes a complex exercise. Nevertheless, the authors have ventured here to create a kind of formula to measure the impact of various technologies relative to the basket of elements that make up the current system. In doing so, we pose the following questions:

- Will implementing a particular technology make the production of energy cleaner?
- Will it make the production and delivery of energy safer?
- Will it make the production and delivery of energy more reliable?
- Will it make energy cheaper to the economy as a whole?

Next we rate the above on a scale of 0–25 and then multiply by (a) the degree to which the technology is proven and (b) the impact the technology can have on our energy infrastructure in the next decade.

So, for example, grid-scale batteries get straight 25 ratings (the highest) in their theoretical ability to make energy cleaner, safer and more reliable, but batteries are very expensive due to their low power density, so they get a 5 for affordability. If these batteries could be installed tomorrow, they would likely have a significant near-term impact, so we give them a 50-percent rating on that score. Sadly, however, the technology remains almost completely unproven: 15 percent. So here goes our simple formula:

$$(25 + 25 + 25 + 5) \times .50 \times .15 = 6$$

The bottom line is that grid-scale batteries, while promising in theory, stand a very low chance of improving our energy infrastructure in the next decade. As you'll see, however, other technologies score 100 points. (For the convenience of readers, the results are presented in a small graphic at the head of relevant chapters.)

It is important to note that these estimates are more back-of-the-envelope than they are definitive. We didn't run them through a supercomputer; they mix matters of fact and opinion. But, at the same time, these figures are not stabs in the dark. They are based upon a great deal of primary-source reading and upon conversations with hundreds of people in the field.

The time has come to sort out our energy options in an organized, if not conclusive, way. We have not reached the end of the debate about our energy future, but neither do we remain at the beginning. It might be fair to say—to paraphrase Winston Churchill—that we are coming to the end of the beginning.

We opened this book with a quote about dreams and responsibilities. As an energy infrastructure investor and an energy industry analyst, as fathers and husbands and Americans, we're completely in favor of dreaming. But to let our dreams capture us rather than capturing our dreams is to pave a road to hell with our own good intentions.

By all means let society encourage scientists and inventors and poets to envision the technologies of the next century or millennium. But hope, as the saying goes, is not a strategy. While we're building a ladder to the stars, we need practical shorter-term technologies to address our increasingly pressing energy challenges down here on earth.

Fortunately, many brilliant people have already delved into their piece of this puzzle and begun to create solutions that will—with encouragement—come online in the not-too-distant future. And even more fortunately, some of these solutions are available to us *right now.* All we need do is beat a path to their door.

Hidden in Plain Sight

For many good reasons, we ask more than ever of our energy suppliers. We want the fuel that they provide to be cleaner, safer, more reliable and cheaper than it is today. And we'd like these qualities to be delivered very soon, if you please.

To achieve these goals, some urge a switch from one fossil fuel to another or the abandonment of fossil fuels altogether. Sometimes in the next breath these same people blame institutional inertia or vested interests or flat-out cynicism for the reluctance of "the system" to make big changes.

But there's more to it than that. The fact is that we might achieve any one or two of the important qualities mentioned above by initiating such a switch, but only, in most cases, at the expense of the other three things that we claim to want.

This problem arises because there are reasons why we have the infrastructure that we do, where fossil fuels provide 90 percent of the horsepower we use. [4] Notwithstanding their shortcomings, these basic inputs grew to dominate the energy economy because they are plentiful, relatively inexpensive and demonstrably reliable. If we are to dream of replacing them *and* maintaining our quality of life, we had better be sure not to throw the baby out with the bathwater.

The good news is that if we want to lower the environmental impact of energy while making it safer, cleaner and more reli-

able, we have the means to do so today without radically elimi-
nating traditional sources of energy and without ratcheting back
our standard of living. Microsoft's Bill Gates has been quoted as
saying that people overestimate the impact of technology looking two years out, but underestimate its impact looking ten years
out. In fact, from a technological perspective, if we begin to
transform our energy infrastructure in the next two years using
existing, proven technology, the impact in a decade will be far
greater than if we undertake to reinvent that infrastructure from
the ground up.

We don't need a Soviet-style Ten-Year Plan to begin making energy better, because many means of doing so exist now.
And they're not buried in a back room of the U.S. Patent Office.
They're hiding in plain sight. The majority of these solutions fall
under the rubric of "energy intelligence." That is, they involve
technological innovation within the current system.

The original build-out of our energy infrastructure—mostly
in the early part of the twentieth century—leveraged economies
of scale. This strategy worked brilliantly given the technology (or
lack thereof) of the time, but that doesn't mean simply applying
more scale—building a million new windmills, say, or replacing
every power plant with a newer version—is the right choice for
our near-term energy future. We live in the Digital Age. Many of
our best options for improvement involve silicon rather than scale.

By making our energy infrastructure more intelligent, we
make it more efficient. From these efficiencies accrue huge
benefits, delivered much more affordably than those that could
derive in the near future from technologies commonly thought
of as Cleantech: biofuels, fuel cells, solar and wind. A demand-
response load switch may not be as photogenic as a windmill
or a solar panel, but it has the benefit of being much less capital intensive while delivering a similar result. Comverge is the
pioneer in reducing electric grid load during periods of peak
demand. Comverge's load switch, which is placed on residen-

tial air conditioners and hot water heaters cost about $300 per kilowatt installed. Solar power costs approximately $6,000 per kilowatt. In 2009, Comverge had 2900 megawatts of capacity installed and under management at approximately 1/20th the cost versus the 2100 megawatts of solar installed nationwide.[5]

One might say that Energy 1.0 was built using economies of scale, while the "hidden Cleantech revolution"—Energy 2.0—stands to improve existing energy systems by unleashing *economies of connection.* When we make our mines, oil fields, power plants and electric grids more intelligent, we achieve the seeming miracle of delivering all four critical attributes that we seek. Thus we make energy cleaner, smarter, more reliable and cheaper. In other words, we make energy better.

Unlike many in the Cleantech community, the authors don't believe a sustainable future requires consuming less of everything and changing human behavior. In fact, the Hidden Cleantech Revolution will enhance our prosperity, increase our consumption of energy and improve our quality of life.

The energy industry has already made huge strides in the right direction, but astonishing gains can still be extracted from our energy infrastructure. This story must be told and understood broadly by energy executives, investors, policy makers and voters.

Six Things to Remember

An appreciation of scale is the logical starting point of any conversation about energy. This book's thesis begins with the following empirical observation:

Our energy infrastructure is vast.

There are 25 congressional committees involved in shaping energy policy, with two dozen federal agencies implementing that policy on behalf of the executive branch. In addition, every state has its own Public Utility Commission—another 50 deliberative bodies weighing in.

What do these 100 regulators and administrators oversee? On the utility side, the asset value of the U.S. electricity infrastructure alone exceeds $800 billion.[6] And among business enterprises, the oil and gas industry contributes roughly $1 trillion annually to U.S. gross domestic product.[7] Even in this age of massive financial bailouts and stimulus packages, $1,000,000,000,000 is a lot of money.

The world adopted fossil fuels for their availability, relative cost, and many qualitative advantages over other options, including energy density and ease of storage. A gigantic infrastructure of ports, pipelines, power lines, substations and filling stations has grown over several generations to accommodate the production, processing, and distribution of oil, gas, coal, and their many derivatives. The roads and highways, carrying roughly 248 million registered vehicles,[8] impose equally considerable constraints on any plans to transition away from our primary energy sources.

This huge infrastructure was built for good reasons. Fossil fuels have powered our prosperity and afforded us the high standard of living that we've come to take for granted. At the same time, their increasing use globally presents risks to this very quality of life. Concerns about health, security, and the environment now lead many to call for a prompt transition to renewable, low-carbon, domestic energy sources.

All else being equal, who wouldn't agree that this transition is desirable? And on this score the trend over the past two centuries is pretty encouraging. We've witnessed a steady de-carbonization of our energy supply, first as we moved from wood to coal, and then from coal to oil. Most scenarios in the literature see this trend persisting in the present century:

For those fearing a climate catastrophe, however, absent

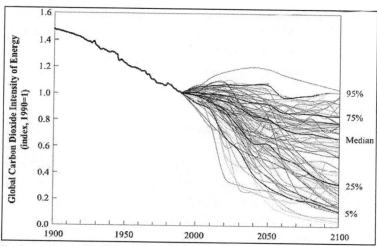

The Past 100 Years has Witnessed a Steady De-Carbonization of Our Energy Sources
Source: Intergovernmental Panel on Climate Change www.ipcc.ch

dramatic immediate reductions in carbon emissions the anticipated pace of transition seems unacceptably slow. The Deepwater Horizon oil spill, which took place right around the time the
authors began working on this book, galvanized new advocates
for renewable energy.

But when media pundits and policy makers call for novel
clean fuel sources to replace oil, they conveniently gloss considerations of scale. In a nation where diesel-fueled vehicles move
94 percent of all goods,[9] wind, solar, and hydrogen can't possibly displace oil as our No. 1 source of transportation energy in
the next decade or two.

The fact is that we've been fretting over the use of fossil
fuels off and on since the Nixon Administration. Why then, do
we still rely on these fuels for 84 percent of our primary energy
supply?[10] Are we so dissolute as a nation that we couldn't adjust
our lifestyles to solve this problem? Are our politicians so cor-
rupted by donations from Big Oil that they won't pull the plug?

These might be convenient assumptions, but they are not
likely telling the whole story—or even most of it. More realisti-

cally, our scant progress to date reflects less a lack of political or personal will than the reality of massive infrastructural inertia, what energy analyst Gregor Macdonald refers to as "the intractability of the built environment."[11] This is a crucial concept, and brings us to our second major observation:

Energy transition is inherently slow.[12]

While the authors take exception to certain justifications for making a clean energy push (competing with China in the manufacture of heavily commoditized solar and wind components, for example), the effort is laudable, and we believe it has legs. It had better, because we're talking about a multi-decade commitment that will stretch far beyond the terms in office of our elected representatives.

The barriers to creating a low-carbon energy system can certainly be overcome in the fullness of time. Energy is as infinite as the human imagination. We've remade the world before and we will do it again. But you can't execute a hairpin turn with an aircraft carrier. We simply will not derive the majority of our electricity, let alone our total primary energy supply, from renewables in 10 or 20 years.[13] To suggest otherwise is irresponsible. It's critical for us to focus on what is really achievable—right now—with the tools at hand. Unrealistic goals are a distraction we can't afford, in terms of both time and resource allocation.

So, what *will* power this effort to decarbonize our energy economy? Strong leadership, technological innovation, an entrepreneurial spirit … and lots of oil, natural gas, coal, and uranium. Because:

The slow transition away from today's dominant fuels will be powered by those same fuels.

We've got a bright future ahead of us. We're going to take significant steps toward decarbonizing our energy supply over the next several decades. Sustained progress will depend upon putting clear, consistent policies into place. We'll also need to ensure that our existing energy systems are up to the task of powering this transition while simultaneously keeping the economic engine humming. Without a strong economy, after all, how are we going to afford any of this?

The bad news is that our massive energy complex currently faces significant stresses. For three decades we have underinvested in transmission and distribution assets, and we are now paying the price as increasing loads stress the electric grid to the point of failure. Meanwhile, our oil supply is challenged by above- and below-ground realities. Coal is economical but presents a host of health and environmental concerns. New nuclear power plants can't seem to get built on time or on budget.

Yet hope is not lost. By targeting investments in each of these areas, we can make our existing energy systems cleaner, safer, more productive, and more reliable. Indeed, we have to if we want to secure our future prosperity. To borrow from G. Steven Farris, CEO of Apache Corporation:

We need to get more out of what we've got.[14]

So how do we make existing sources of energy better? For our money (and we mean that quite literally), the lowest cost, lowest risk, highest return-on-investment commitments that we can undertake as a society and as individual investors are those that make our infrastructure smarter. A smarter grid is more reliable. A smarter oil field is more productive. A smarter coal plant is cleaner. A smarter nuclear plant is safer. These results can all be achieved through innovations in Cleantech.

What exactly is Cleantech? Lux Research defines it as "the universe of innovative technologies designed to optimize the use of natural resources and reduce environmental impact." Solar panels and wind turbines are among the most visible products of the Cleantech revolution, but they can't possibly have the same impact as less visible Cleantech approaches that provide incremental improvements in oil recovery or coal emissions. The latter widely distributed Cleantech opportunities, though immense as a result of the existing installed base, have been overshadowed by the popular discourse over finding new fuel sources. But in fact:

The Hidden Cleantech Revolution is the bigger story.

This revolution has energy productivity at its core. A 2007 McKinsey study (one of whose authors is now senior advisor to the Secretary of Energy) found that currently available productivity-boosting technologies offering a positive rate of return could shave 116 to 173 quadrillion BTU, or 19 to 28 percent, off of projected world energy demand in 2020. By contrast, non-hydro renewable power sources moving from 2 percent to 5 percent of the world's energy supply, combined with biofuels jumping from one percent to 10 percent of the global fuel mix, would add only 30 "quads" to the primary energy supply.[15]

Information Technology has transformed practically every aspect of American life, from education to entertainment. And, on the surface, energy is a decidedly high-technology business. But I.T. has not penetrated the sector nearly as deeply as it could.

These changes have indeed begun to happen, however. Today's refineries are a perfect example of I.T.'s ability to layer intelligence on top of existing infrastructure and extract tremendous value. Dumb devices, implanted with silicon chips and networked together, collectively become very smart.[16] The implementation of this strategy is akin to harvesting low-hanging fruit.

Intelligence, as embedded in hardware and software, lies at the core of many of the solutions the authors will discuss in this book. Compared to completely new infrastructure, these are relatively capital-light investments, and they can leverage the massive installed base of existing infrastructure. Remember:

Silicon scales much better than steel.

The sorts of investments this book focuses on also play to our strength as a nation. In today's heavily networked, information-based economy, it's not economies of *scale* that dominate, but economies of *connection*. Network effects are a formidable economic force. Don't think Andrew Carnegie. Think eBay or Google or American Express. Google, which was founded in 1998, has a larger market capitalization than the five largest U.S. utilities *combined*.

A network of devices in communication with one another— the so-called Internet of Things[17]—is something the energy business certainly needs to harness. It also needs to focus on networks of people. How can a far-flung group of oil and gas professionals better collaborate to come up with an optimal well design? How can multibillion dollar projects involving thousands of workers be managed so that the right information is accessible to the right people, moving the project forward safely, on time, and on budget?

In these pages, we'll see examples of innovations ported over to the energy space from the military, from aeronautical engineering, and from other diverse areas. Technology isn't nearly as much about new gadgets as it is about creating new combinations of existing components through architectural innovation. As in the case of Henry Ford bringing the meatpacking disassembly line to the automotive assembly line, such recombinations often require looking outside one's own business framework.

That brings us to a major reason we're writing this book. There are plenty of trade shows filled with entrepreneurs seeking money and professional gatherings filled with engineers seeking deeper understanding. But we've searched in vain for a dedicated forum where industry professionals, entrepreneurs, and enthusiasts can get together and cross-pollinate ideas for improving existing energy systems. That's the sort of interaction this short book intends to foster.

As energy investors, we've come across many compelling technologies and solutions. We'll share some of those with you in the following pages and we'll rate their near-term viability based upon the formula we discussed in the introduction. It's a purposefully brief survey of what we see happening out there, but one that we hope will encourage the reader to share his or her own ideas and experiences with us—and, more important, with one another.

Our thesis is that there are five priorities we need to pursue to cost effectively secure America's energy future. We need to play offense and get more out of the grid, oil and gas, coal, nuclear. We also need to play defense and invest in the safety, security and resilience of our infrastructure. We are not arguing that one of these is a higher priority than the other. We should think about our energy choices as a portfolio. We need diversity but we also need to understand the "Hidden Cleantech Revolution" that is happening today without government subsidies to choose the lowest cost, lowest risk and highest return investments to secure our future.

Visit the website www.hiddenCleantech.com and post your comments or start a new section. Give the technologies your own ratings. Let us know what we missed and what companies we should mention in the next edition. Reach out to the enterprises in this book to learn more about their solutions. The connections among energy technologists, investors and policy makers represent our nation's true wealth.

NATIONAL PRIORITY
Getting More from the Grid

T he American electric grid should be counted among the wonders of the modern world. As related in Jason Makansi's insightful book *Lights Out*, "our electricity system can be considered one huge machine."[18] Measured by route miles and physical footprint, the North American electric grid is the second largest network on the planet, after our roads and highways.[19] Following the path of least resistance, electricity zips along the transmission and distribution (T&D) network, often traveling hundreds of miles and crossing multiple state lines on its journey.

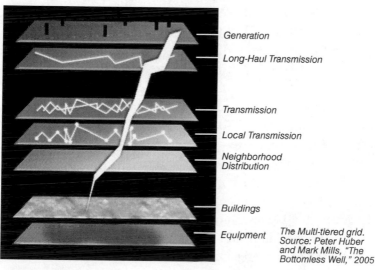

Generation

Long-Haul Transmission

Transmission

Local Transmission

Neighborhood Distribution

Buildings

Equipment

The Multi-tiered grid. Source: Peter Huber and Mark Mills, "The Bottomless Well," 2005

In 2003, the National Academy of Engineering ranked the top 20 engineering achievements of the twentieth century. Automobiles, airplanes, computers, and many other marvels made the list, but electrification came out on top.[20] Perhaps a rare few Americans paid attention to these rankings, however. The rest of us went about our daily business, as aware of electricity as we are of the oxygen that we breathe.

Ironically, 2003 was also the year of the Northeast Blackout, which affected roughly 50 million people. That event cost the economy between $4 and $10 billion.[21] In some areas of the U.S., power remained out for four days, surprising millions who had come to depend upon the reliability of the electric grid. But what surprises many experts on that subject is not the fact that the whole Northeast lost power in one fell swoop on a hot summer day. Rather, they wonder why we haven't had many more such widespread disruptions.

From 1960 to 1980, the United States experienced a major building boom of electrical infrastructure. During this period electric rates increased dramatically across the country. But in the past 40 years we have substantially de-capitalized the grid. As a result, we now have the lowest inflation-adjusted cost of electricity in 50 years, along with a grid that's falling apart. This is about to change.

Eric Eggers, Energy Analyst for Credit Suisse, in a recent presentation to the Aspen Institute projected that U.S. utilities must spend $1 trillion in the next 20 years to meet renewable portfolio standards, build new transmission capacity, and replace aging fossil fuel plants.[22] To pay for these essential upgrades, our electric bills will have to double from today's level unless we can figure out another solution.

Right now our grid is mostly old-tech or, if you will, pretty dumb. In fact, when you consider that the North American electric grid is the biggest, most complicated networked machine in the world, its "dumbness" is amazing. The grid is essentially still an analog system feeding power to our digital world. A 2009 Department of Energy (DOE) survey found that only 28 percent of electric-grid substations were automated and only 46 percent had any form of outage detection. The same study determined that 80 percent of relays were electromechanical, while only 20 percent were digital.[23] This lack of intelligence is why *you* have to call the utility when your power goes out.

IBM recently published a smart grid report calling attention to the monitoring gap that exists between transmission lines and commercial and residential electric meters. How does the average utility calculate how much capacity they have available? They work off of historical models and the nameplate capacity of transformers and overhead lines. In other words, they read their old records, read the labels on their equipment, and make their best guess.

To compensate for lack of knowledge they have to build in a reserve margin of safety that is typically 18–20 percent of the nameplate capacity. But their lack of situational awareness isn't so easily overcome. It leads to even bigger inefficiencies.

For example, ambient heat stresses electrical grid components and reduces their real capacity, while breezes or cold temperatures increases their capacity; but the dumb grid has no way to adjust itself to these changes. Real-time monitoring of transformers and overhead lines would enable central station electric grid operators to increase the throughput of the grid and reduce its reserve margin by up to half—to 9–10 percent. That's equivalent to over $100 billion of avoided capacity cost and unnecessary transmission and generation. From an environmental perspective, it would provide the means to grow the grid by 10 percent without adding a molecule of additional carbon to the air.[24]

Our Stressed-Out Transmission Network

Consumption of electricity in the United States has increased 300 percent since 1975, primarily due to the proliferation of power-hungry consumer products and computers.[25]

As the grid gets pushed harder than ever, managers increase "wheeling" of electricity across great distances. But, meanwhile, long-term growth of transmission capacity has dramatically failed to keep pace with the growth of peak demand. If current trends continue, forecasters predict there will be less than a one percent increase in total miles of transmission cables by 2012.[26]

So-called transmission loading relief (TLR) procedures are one means of heading off excessive congestion by grid reliability coordinators. Here's a chart of "Level 5b" (the most serious, short of emergency-level) TLR procedures in recent years:

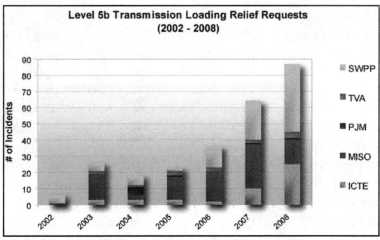

The Level of Loading Relief Requests is Rising. Source: North American Electric Reliability Corporation www.nerc.com

When crisis hits, the great strength of the grid's interconnectedness becomes a great weakness. As the 2003 blackout showed, localized events (caused by accidents, equipment failure or a terrorist attack) can rapidly cascade into large-scale outages.

As one might expect given the above facts, power outages

and interruptions, which cost the country about $100 billion per year,[27] have been on the rise.

One response to our stressed-out grid would be to build a lot of new long-distance transmission lines. Some, like financier T. Boone Pickens, envision a "super grid" linking new wind and solar farms to distant population centers. But resistance to this approach is bound to be significant given most people's reluctance to welcome new transmission lines in their backyards. Every mile of proposed transmission represents a potential lawsuit from aggrieved landowners and environmental groups.

Our needs march on, however. Economic and population growth demand more energy. And our electronic lifestyles demand not just more, but purer electricity.

Power quality incidents before the Digital Age were difficult to diagnose due to short interruption periods. In the old days, a partial restoration of power (or brownout) resulted in light bulbs being half lit. Now the digital revolution has increased the stakes. A partial restoration of power won't run appliances like computers or routers, so the increase in power-sensitive appliances and digital load requirements has forced us to more narrowly define power quality. For example, ten years ago "voltage sags" might be classified by the utility as drops of 40 percent or more for 60 cycles. Today a 15 percent drop for five cycles constitutes a voltage sag.[28]

Further complicating matters, due to inefficiencies the United States loses in excess of 1.65 trillion kilowatt hours (kWh) per year—1 trillion in long-distance transmission and 650 billion throughout the distribution system. The dissipation of this energy has serious consequences. It leads to wasted electricity, unnecessary power generation, lost money, and millions of tons of unnecessary CO_2 being spewed into the atmosphere.

If adopted with decisiveness, efficiency technologies hold

out the hope of mitigating these challenges in a major way over the next decade. According to electrical component giant ABB, just a ten percent improvement in the efficiency of the distribution grid would save almost $6 billion and reduce carbon emissions by 42 million tons.[29]

The following technologies and processes might help us achieve that goal and more.

Chapter 2

Dynamic Rating

Clean Score	Safety Score	Reliability Score	Affordability Score	X Degree Proven	X Likely Near-term Impact	TOTAL SCORE
25	15	25	25	100%	75%	67.5

W hen we say we want to leverage silicon rather than steel, we don't mean the silicon in solar cells. Silicon is our shorthand for the chips and fibers that increasingly extend the reach of our networked economy into every object out there. The smart grid layers inexpensive digital monitors on the old analog grid to extend its life and enable us to get more out of those assets that we can't afford to replace.

As we mentioned in the overview above, one cause of electric grid inefficiency has been the inability of utilities to make smart adjustments to variations in wire temperature and other field variables. The high-tech process that can give them this almost instantaneous capability is known as "dynamic rating."

To employ dynamic rating, utilities must first install monitoring instruments that measure the real-time sag and temperature of their transmission cables. With dynamic rating of a transmission line using a device like GridSense's LineTracker, the operator can afford to be less conservative and confidently transfer more electricity without thermally overloading the line.

Once this equipment is in place, dynamic rating increases line utilization by allowing existing delivery infrastructure to operate closer to true capacity limits. Dynamic line ratings have the potential to provide at least an additional 10 to 15 percent transmission capacity 95 percent of the time.[30]

The Gridsense LineTracker®
Source: Gridsense

Dynamic rating affords an enormous opportunity. Currently only a small fraction of the nation's transmission lines are monitored this way. Specifically, the July 2009 Smart Grid System report by the DOE judged that only 0.3 percent of utility transmission lines were dynamically rated.[31]

Think: *Installing Dynamic Rating equipment on 100 percent of American power lines would free up as much as 7% of our electric capacity and eliminate building $70 Billion of new power plants.*[32]

Chapter 3

Smart Meters

Clean Score	Safety Score	Reliability Score	Affordability Score	X Degree Proven	X Likely Near-term Impact	TOTAL SCORE
0	0	5	5	100%	75%	7.5

The Brattle Group estimates that fully building a smart grid by 2030 will be a $1.5 to $2 trillion endeavor. The front end of that build-out involves around $900 billion in spending on communications infrastructure (hardware and software) that largely falls under the rubric of advanced metering infrastructure (AMI).[33]

Last October, President Obama announced $3.4 billion in grant awards for grid modernization, and AMI snagged the lion's share.[34] As the backbone for all of the enhancements to come, AMI's early prominence is unsurprising.

One of the most high-profile smart grid applications linked to AMI is the "smart" two-way meter. The electric meters most of us still have today record little more than customer usage. Smart meters add the following attributes:

- Automated remote meter reading
- Outage detection
- Time-of-use billing
- "Net" metering, where the customer sells power back to the utility

These days there's so much enthusiasm for smart meters among investors that one midsized manufacturer, Itron, was recently valued at approximately *60 times* trailing earnings. Utilities also seem happy enough to make these investments, which sport a six-year payback, according to Computer Sciences Corporation.[35]

For large commercial customers who are heavy users of electricity, smart meters have merits, too. But friction comes into the equation on the small-business and residential customer side. For the average residential user, electricity is ideally invisible. Statistics show that she spends six to nine minutes per year interacting with her utility, generally only when something goes wrong.[36] Does this person want to think more about her power usage, monitoring real-time pricing trends throughout the day and responding to that information by adjusting her demand? Unlikely.

Furthermore, although so far smart meter programs have been pitched as a money-saving opportunity for customers, there's no reason time-of-use pricing can't have the opposite effect. If the point is to increase efficiency overall, higher utility bills are perfectly acceptable to an economist, but early residential users aren't taking that lightly. In fact, the AARP has voiced strong opposition to mandatory participation in smart meter programs,[37] which are being challenged by high-profile lawsuits in California and Texas.[38]

As long as a utility's business model is tied to selling more juice, there will be skepticism that utilities genuinely want to help their customers to conserve electricity.[39] It will take awhile to drive this so-called decoupling forward.[40] A major game changer could be more residential solar, wind or a significant percentage of Americans charging their electric vehicles in their garages and selling excess power back to the grid. But these factors are a long way off because of the huge investment required by consumers and the current poor return on that investment.

So while there's a great deal of buzz surrounding the "smart grid" today, two-way meters and time-of-use pricing tend to steal the spotlight. As we'll discuss in upcoming chapters, there are hidden developments going on in this space that may trump smart meters in significance in the near term.

Chapter 4

Distribution Automation

Clean Score	Safety Score	Reliability Score	Affordability Score	X Degree Proven	X Likely Near-term Impact	TOTAL SCORE
25	25	25	25	90%	90%	81

ccidents will happen. When it comes to critical infrastructure protection, the goal must be resilience: the ability to withstand and recover from adversity. The grid will do this better if we implement technologies that enable it to evolve from reactionary management of the network to proactive and predictive systems.

Despite some obvious shortcomings, there's already a good amount of resilience built into our electricity infrastructure. Almost by definition the interconnected network offers redundancy, which means that an outage at any particular point is generally no big deal. In addition, many utility operators have situational awareness not only through angry phone calls from customers, but also through monitoring via SCADA (supervisory control and data acquisition) networks.

One component of these networks, the so-called Intelligent Electronic Device (historically of a mechanical nature), detects faults and automatically trips switchgear to block the flow of fault current. But even adoption of "Smart Grid 1.0"—a relatively low-tech solution more commonly known as the utilities' Distribution Management System (DMS)—has lagged. Though it's been around for decades, today only 17 percent of utilities have a DMS system.[41]

Smart Grid 2.0 consists of real-time two-way communication and predictive analytics within a utility's transmission and distribution infrastructure, making it more proactive and therefore more adaptive. In this scenario, decisions become decentralized and get pushed out to transformers and overhead lines— that is, to the edges of the network, closer to potential trouble. Thus managers can identify at-risk equipment before it fails, pre-empting disruptive events. If outages do occur, the system automatically isolates and corrects them much faster and more reliably than under a centralized supervisory system.

EXPANDING CAPACITY WHILE EXTENDING AGING ASSETS

One major advantage of spreading two-way sensors and communications devices throughout the grid is the ability to expand the capacity of the assets through dynamic rating, which enables a utility to load transformers and overhead lines beyond their nameplate capacity, sometimes increasing throughput up to 10–20 percent beyond what is possible through static thermal loading guides without undue risk.

From a business perspective, this is particularly important because on a hot summer day the real-time price of power due to congestion can spike from $40 per kWh to a maximum of $2000 per kWh, making the return on investment spectacular for any expansion of throughput. More important, from a reliability perspective technologies of this nature will be increasingly essential to keeping the lights on.

In the near term, transformer monitoring is one extremely useful function of a smarter T&D system, given the average age of the installed base of this critical equipment. For example, over

20 percent of American Electric Power's operating transformers are beyond their life expectancy.[42]

Across companies, new installations peaked in 1973–74. Now, 35 years later, that generation of equipment is headed for an exponential increase in failures.[43] Fortunately, 80 percent of those are predictable within the framework of a distribution-automated system, according to Eaton Corporation, which sells a device that monitors the partial discharge of gases that is a symptom of insulation degradation—a leading cause of some of the most frequent and costly failures.[44]

GridSense has its own versatile, low-cost transformer monitoring solution. Called TransformerIQ, it watches up to 24 different failure points on a transformer. The addition of this $3,000 monitoring device can help extend the life of a $300,000 transformer and, in the process, improve the grid's reliability. In effect, TranformerIQ has the potential to extend an operator's "vision" into tens of thousands of distribution transformers in the utility's network. This better enables the utility to predict the remaining life of its equipment and to ascertain the real-time loading and routing of power, leading to better decisions and improving system reliability.

The Gridsense Transformer IQ® Source: Gridsense

THE SELF-HEALING GRID

Wide-area monitoring systems are another key to better asset awareness and reliability enhancement. With the use of devices called phasor measurement units (PMUs), or synchrophasors, utilities can get a much clearer picture of the condition of the grid in something much closer to real time. GPS is the key enabling technology, as only satellite clocks are accurate enough to synchronize measurements being taken 30 times per second. The CEO of PJM Interconnection—the largest regional transmission system in North America—describes the switch to synchrophasors this way: "It's like moving from an old black-and-white TV to a wide-screen HD TV."[45]

The old way of doing business was using forensic tools to figure out what went wrong on transmission lines after a blackout. PMUs, in contrast, provide active monitoring tools that can prevent blackouts from occurring in the first place. According to a 2004 study from the DOE, wide-area measurement systems could have eliminated the $4.5 billion of losses that resulted from the 2003 blackout in the Northeast. Investing millions to save the economy billions in avoided outages? That sounds like money well spent.[46]

Regulators are catching on. Observing this technology, Jeanne Fox, a New Jersey Board of Public Utilities Commissioner, said, "The self-healing grid is a beautiful thing. The payback will be quick and the reliability is better."[47]

FACTS

Transmission organizations in California and Texas plan on using phasor data to better monitor intermittent generation from sources like solar and wind power.[48] Another useful tool for integrating intermittent sources is a so-called FACTS (Flexible AC Transmission System) device. This piece of electronic equipment provides critical voltage and power flow control, which ensures both reliability and maximum output from a wind-energy interconnection.

Renewables integration is just one feature to recommend FACTS technology. Voltage reduction is also a key weapon in a utility's arsenal when it comes to relieving grid congestion. (We'll take a look at a second, demand response, in the next chapter.) By rerouting electricity away from congested areas at times of peak demand, FACTS installations allow for improved grid reliability, control, and capacity. ABB, a global leader in the manufacture of power equipment, reports that FACTS devices alone can enhance transmission capacity by an astonishing 20 to 40 percent.[49]

The technology has been refined for several decades. Today General Electric says these systems can be installed at a fraction of the cost of building new transmission lines, and typically have a payback period of *less than two years.*[50] Equally amazing, although there are now close to 90 FACTS installations in the U.S., that number represents a tiny fraction of the total market potential.[51]

We hope more utility executives will educate themselves about the value proposition of FACTS in particular and distribution automation in general.[52]

Consider: *Installing economical monitoring solutions on every transformer in America costs less than constructing a single 300 megawatt gas-fired power plant.*[53]

Chapter 5

Demand Response

Clean Score	Safety Score	Reliability Score	Affordability Score	X Degree Proven	X Likely Near-term Impact	TOTAL SCORE
25	10	25	25	100%	100%	85

E lectricity is one of the few commodities that cannot be stored. Supply and demand must always balance, and any significant imbalance can cause voltage disturbances or even a blackout. As a result, the value of a traveling electron greatly depends upon its location at any given point in time. On a summer day during the hottest point of the afternoon, the price of electricity can skyrocket versus the price that same morning or evening.

Utilities have several ways to deal with these supply and demand imbalances. On the supply side a utility can buy merchant power to supplement its base-load nuclear and coal plants. Merchant power plants are most often gas "peakers," called such because they may run as little as 80 hours per year. Do the math and you'll understand why, when these facilities do run, their owners are very well paid.

Another approach is called demand response. In this scenario, the utility offers an incentive to its residential and commercial customers to curtail demand during peaks. During a period of peak demand, reducing the consumption of a single appliance has little value. But reducing the demand of 90,000 appliances in a small city can help prevent a blackout or eliminate the cost of the utility having to purchase expensive merchant power. In a world where everything is connected—down to the smallest device—we will have the ability to aggregate individual consuming units like water heaters, air conditioning units, washers and dryers into a whole that has tremendous value.

The leader in residential demand response is Comverge, which uses public pager networks to send signals to load switches installed on residential appliances. The power of demand response comes from its low cost, scalability and ease of deployment. A Comverge load switch costs approximately $300 installed and can throttle back about one kilowatt of power. Comverge already has networks of over five million homes throughout the United States. In these networks, the company's load switches remotely reduce the electricity consumption of their customers' air conditioners when needed. This allows utilities to "cycle" residential and small commercial and industrial air conditioners, reducing load at peak times.

In Salt Lake City and a few other communities, 35 percent of homes already have a Comverge load switch, helping to control their air conditioners' electricity consumption. By the end of 2009, Comverge owned or was managing load switches affecting about 2,900 megawatts of power.[35] By comparison, U.S. solar electric installed capacity totaled around 2,100 megawatts that year.[36]

EnerNOC is the leader in commercial demand response. The company uses backup diesel and gas generators to shed load from their commercial customers in order to help utilities shave peak demand.

Another player in this field is the so-called "electricity curtailment provider." These companies help manage demand by paying large electricity users (such as steel mills) to take electricity-hogging equipment (such as electric furnaces) off-line during periods of peak demand.

Demand response is one of the lowest-cost, highest-return investments that a utility can make. In addition, by "layering intelligence" onto the existing grid utilities can avoid building costly new power generation and transmission lines.

The authors are constantly on the lookout for the next Comverge: a high-value, off-the-shelf solution that's hidden in plain sight.

Imagine: *For the same cost of running 3,000 miles of new high voltage power lines (less than four percent of the installed base) we could put one power-saving load switch on every household's central air conditioning system in America.*[54]

Chapter 6

Smart Vegetation Management

Clean Score	Safety Score	Reliability Score	Affordability Score	X Degree Proven	X Likely Near-term Impact	TOTAL SCORE
13	9	25	25	100%	100%	72

The first advertisement for bids to provide utility poles ran in a Washington, D.C., newspaper. It read in part: "Sealed proposals will be received by the undersigned for furnishing 700 straight and sound chestnut posts with the bark on and of the following dimensions to wit: 'Each post must not be less than eight inches in diameter at the butt and tapering to five or six inches at the top. Six hundred and eighty of said posts to be 24 feet in length, and 20 of them 30 feet in length.'"

The date was February 7, 1844, and the undersigned was Samuel Morse.[55]

Ever since then, presumably, utilities have had to contend with the nuisance of vegetation growing up poles or interfering with overhead wires. Yet, amazingly, the North American Electric Reliability Corporation (NERC), the self-regulatory organization for electric reliability, only began collecting vegetation-related outage information in 2004, after one cause of the Northeast Blackout was determined to be failure by Ohio utility

FirstEnergy to trim trees in its transmission rights-of-way.[56]

Given the scale of the electric grid, it should be no surprise that vegetation management is a big-time business, with market leader Asplundh Tree Expert Company doing over $2.5 billion in annual sales, according to Hoover's.[57] One might be tempted to think that tree trimming is a low-tech and straightforward affair, but it turns out that Asplundh leverages Information Technology in some interesting ways.

A LOCATION-BASED BOOST

From Kevin Kelly, we've learned that "the surest way to smartness is through massive dumbness."[58] Kelly's example was the delivery of wet cement by Mexico's Cemex, whose adoption of GPS technology allowed the company's drivers to form a decentralized, intelligent swarm much more effective than a traditional dispatch system. With the new system Cemex achieved on-time delivery rates of roughly 98 percent, compared to 35 percent previously.

Asplundh has taken similar steps, linking up with location-based services provider Telogis to automate and improve its fleet management using GPS. Asplundh cites half a dozen different benefits from the rollout of this program, from more efficient routing to improved driver safety.[59] Telogis has found that its routing efficiency solution alone can offer a 3-year ROI of 690 percent.[60] You don't get that kind of return by simply adding another truck to your fleet.

While GPS keeps the trucks operating efficiently on the road, another technology, called LiDAR (Light Detection and Ranging), makes sure they set their priorities straight.

Traditional vegetation management requires thousands of hours of ground observation combined with guesswork about things such as the distance between a power line and nearby trees, and how that line might sag when wind-driven limbs make contact with it. Asplundh has improved its situational awareness with LiDAR, which uses a helicopter equipped with a precise navigation system and a scanning laser. The equipment provides measurements of relative positioning that are accurate to plus or minus six inches, and the resulting map enables the company to prioritize trimming of those lines that are most vulnerable.[61]

In the words of a vegetation manager for BCHydro, the third-largest electric utility in Canada, LiDAR combined with line-design software "has the potential to become the most significant development in right-of-way vegetation management since the invention of the chain saw."[62]

Think: *Reducing vegetation-related outages by 50 percent would save enough energy to remove two 1,000 megawatt power plants from the grid.*[63]

Chapter 7

Energy Storage

Clean Score	Safety Score	Reliability Score	Affordability Score	X Degree Proven	X Likely Near-term Impact	TOTAL SCORE
25	25	25	5	50%	15%	6

lectricity is an amazingly useful and flexible form of power, but storing it in large amounts is about as easy as catching lightning in a bottle. Centralized grid storage has long been possible using mechanisms such as pumped storage (i.e. sending water uphill when power is cheap and abundant and running it back down through a turbine when demand is high), but what we really need is more *distributed* energy storage. That means batteries—very large batteries. National Energy Technology Lab (NETL—the technology arm of the Department of Energy) has identified advanced batteries as "the smart grid's killer application."[64]

Any vision of a world powered by renewable energy rests heavily on advances in grid storage. In the foreseeable future, according to NETL, "it is possible that, with the addition of sufficient energy storage, the penetration of renewables can be significantly above 20 percent." The implication is that we are going to remain roughly 80 percent reliant on nonrenewables without major advances in energy storage technology.

43

Current advanced battery solutions include sodium sulfur (NAS), vanadium redox (VRB), zinc bromide (ZnBr), and lithium ion (Li-ion), but none of these technologies currently achieves the needed scale. Industrial giants Siemens and United Technologies are promoting molten salt technology as a heat collection mechanism in solar thermal power plants. By potentially extending the operations of a plant to 24 hours, whether or not the sun is shining, this technology could do wonders for solar's relatively low capacity factor.[65] This technology has been deployed by Enel at its Archimede plant in Sicily, which is well worth watching.[66]

As for grid-scale batteries used to store electrical energy, they hold great promise, as they have for as long as we can remember. Bill Gates, who's recently emerged as an energy research-and-development evangelist, says we need a battery that's a factor of 100 better than what we have now.[67] The speed of progress in this area is difficult to handicap, but given the history of battery development, such exponential growth could take decades.

Sadly, energy storage is easily one of the most overhyped areas of Cleantech. While the authors salute the scientists and engineers hard at work on this vexing challenge, it behooves investors, utility executives, and policymakers to manage their expectations.

Did You Know: *Gasoline holds 80 times as many watt hours per kilogram as a lithium-ion battery. This is why affordability is a significant hurdle to widespread adoption versus conventional use of fossil fuels.*[68]

NATIONAL PRIORITY
Getting More from
Oil and Gas

In 2008, oil and natural gas accounted for over 60 percent of primary energy consumption in the United States.[69] (Oil is No. 1 by a good margin, and coal lags natural gas by a smidge). While natural gas may rise in prominence relative to oil in the future, the fact remains that this hydrocarbon duo will be powering America for decades to come.

An increasingly popular view, championed by arch-druids and industry veterans alike, is that global flow rates of oil are approaching or have already surpassed their peak. Mature fields are declining, while discoveries of new "supergiant" fields have dwindled.

These are major challenges, and it's hard to predict what technical innovations could stave off the coming crude crunch. But innovations do come. Economist Paul Romer, speaking broadly about economic growth, put this best when he said: "Every generation has perceived the limits to growth that finite resources and undesirable side effects would pose if no new recipes or ideas were discovered. And every generation has underestimated the potential for finding new recipes and ideas. We consistently fail to grasp how many ideas remain to be discovered. Possibilities do not add up. They multiply."[70]

He may as well have been talking about the history of energy discovery. The shale gas bonanza is just the latest in a long string of unexpected surprises that have kept the volatile fossil fuel industry vibrant. While no one can say exactly where the next breakthrough energy discovery or innovation will come from, it's a safe bet that another one *will* come for the simple reason that it always has before. Such is the course of human progress, which is Romer's point.

In the following chapters, we'll take a quick look back at a past development that dramatically changed the exploration game. We'll then turn our sights to the real prize, and to some technology applications that will likely help to secure adequate supplies of oil in the decades ahead. Next, we'll review shale fracturing, which in a short time has totally changed the outlook for natural gas. Finally, we'll present our vision of the digital oil field.

Chapter 8

Seismic
Exploration

Clean Score	Safety Score	Reliability Score	Affordability Score	X Degree Proven	X Likely Near-term Impact	TOTAL SCORE
25	25	25	25	100%	100%	100

A s one might expect, the science of oil and gas exploration was pretty spotty in the early days. Charlatans charged landowners handsome sums to walk around their property with a dubious contraption called a doodlebug, which sought signs of recoverable deposits in Ouija-like fashion. It's a colorful part of oil industry lore, and geophysicists still identify themselves as doodlebuggers. They also continue to call these vast deposits "fossil fuels," though we've known for some time that they don't come from dead dinosaurs.

More scientifically, in the 1920s, the industry successfully began using a device called a reflection seismograph to find commercial-scale deposits. Using dynamite, oil explorers would send small shockwaves into the ground in order to measure the time it took the waves to reflect back, thus gleaning insights into subsurface structures.

Although the reflection seismograph discovered more oil than the original doodlebuggers ever did, it's a crude instrument by today's standards. Indeed, the history of oil exploration is largely the story of geologists learning to see below the earth's surface with increasing accuracy.

Seismic Meets the Supercomputer

In the 1950s, a Conoco team developed Vibroseis technology, a mechanical replacement for dynamite that opened up drilling frontiers that otherwise would have remained off limits. Two-dimensional seismic also came into widespread use around this time, allowing a string of geophone recorders (or towed hydrophones in marine surveys) to image vertical cross-sections of the earth.

Seismic processing hooked up with the budding information revolution in the late 1950s and 1960s and became one of the primary focuses of early supercomputing efforts. Oil exploration has been pushing the limits of computing power ever since.

The new supercomputers allowed the acquisition of three-dimensional seismic data from 1967 onward.[71] Whereas 2-D seismic would record a series of widely spaced vertical cross sections, 3-D could render a much denser and more complete picture of the subsurface. Data acquisition capabilities raced far ahead of the industry's ability to interpret and exploit that data, however. For example, it took one month to shoot an early 3-D survey in New Mexico and two years to process the half-million input traces.[72] Someone had to innovate to close that gap, and someone did.

When H. Roice Nelson was a geophysicist at Mobil Oil, standard industry practice was to print out 2-D cross-sections and mark them up with colored pencils. Nelson concluded that colored pencils wouldn't cut it in the future. 3-D would require a new visualization tool—a graphics workstation—to put the coming torrent of survey data into interpretable form. He quit Mobil to work on this problem.

SEEING OIL IN THREE DIMENSIONS

Nelson hooked up with physicist John Mouton (whom we'll meet again in our look at shale gas), Andy Hildebrand (who later invented the audio pitch-correction software Auto-Tune), and marketing wiz Bob Limbaugh to found a company called Landmark Graphics in 1982. Mouton and Hildebrand thought they should tackle the huge 2-D market first, but Nelson insisted that 3-D was the place to begin. He was proved right: 2-D work processes were deeply entrenched and would only be supplanted after the visualization system for 3-D applications proved itself.

At first, the industry met this new technology with skepticism. The Landmark guys were repeatedly told that the industry had already shot a bunch of surveys and wouldn't pursue many more in the future, the idea being that the data had reached the limits of its usefulness. Of course, as frequently happens, this prediction proved entirely wrong. Before too long, Royal Dutch Shell adopted the technology, and the rest of the majors followed.

Landmark (acquired by Halliburton in the mid-'90s for over half a billion dollars)[73] and its 3-D graphics workstation proved to be key enablers of the 3-D seismic revolution that would follow. The amount of raw data coming in with each survey increased by a factor of 5,000 over the span of 15 years,[74] and digitization and advanced visualization translated this data into better results with the drill bit.

In the 1970s, when the odds of striking oil in a new field were worse than 1 in 5, the term "success rate" seemed like a misnomer.[75] But 20 years later, thanks to the new technology, these rates improved by roughly 50 percent in the United States.[76] And as the technology continued to advance, success rates improved in tandem.

Amoco's success rate jumped from 13 percent in 1991 to 47

percent in 1997.[77] Also by the end of that decade, Zilkha Energy, a small early adopter that the *New York Times* described as a "virtual oil company" on account of its data-driven prospect-generation business model, racked up a 66 percent success rate across 79 wells in the Gulf of Mexico, which had previously come to be called The Dead Sea by wildcatters.[78] Today, explorers like Tullow Oil report success rates that were once unthinkable: 77 percent in 2008 and 87 percent in 2009.[79]

The oil business has a reputation for being a slow adopter of new technology, but once something is a proven moneymaker— well, hang on to your ten-gallon hat. In 1989, 5 percent of the wells drilled in the Gulf of Mexico used 3-D seismic imaging. By 1996, that number leaped to 80 percent.[80] Meanwhile, survey costs plummeted apace.

The explosion of 3-D seismic also has been a major (though hardly the sole) enabler for deepwater exploration, which before 1985 sported a 10 percent success rate. By 2002, the global average was running around 30 percent.[81] Just seven years later, Anadarko Petroleum racked up a 50 percent success rate in its deepwater program, netting it Platts' "Energy Company of the Year" award for 2009.[82]

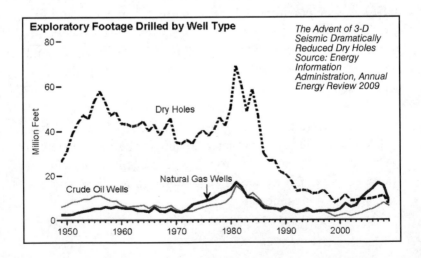

Exploratory Footage Drilled by Well Type

The Advent of 3-D Seismic Dramatically Reduced Dry Holes Source: Energy Information Administration, Annual Energy Review 2009

So, seismic technology has become extremely sophisticated, but it still has room to run. In the near-term future, increasingly dense data acquisition will push resolutions higher, and engineers will integrate the technology with complementary imaging techniques, such as controlled-source electromagnetics. Better subterranean imaging will help pinpoint major new deepwater deposits, and time-lapse seismic will literally add a whole new dimension.

RESERVE GROWTH

Exploration plays a critical role in the oil supply equation and will continue to do so, but consider the following statistic: for the decade running from 1993 to 2002, 75 percent of global liquid reserve additions came *not* from new field discoveries, but from *revisions and extensions of known accumulations*.[83] This is the key factor that allowed reserves to keep up with the growth of world consumption in recent decades.

Furthermore, absent a stunning breakthrough on the exploration front, the authors expect revision and extension to account for the majority of growth in reserves for the remainder of the oil era. Apache Corporation's experience in the United Kingdom's North Sea clearly illustrates this broad trend.

Apache, one of America's leading "independents" (meaning they lack the integration and heft of a major like Chevron), took the Forties field off BP's hands in 2003. Forties is the largest field ever discovered in the U.K. North Sea, but at the time of the sale it was considered a "fading star."[84] Production had declined from 70,000 barrels per day in 2000 to around 40,000 barrels per day before Apache took over—more than a 40 percent decline in seven years.[85]

Despite this profile, by the end of 2005 Apache had nearly *doubled* production at Forties *and* added around *80 million bar-*

rels of proven reserves. Furthermore, the firm determined that the field had perhaps 800 million more barrels of original oil in place than BP had thought.[86]

Somewhere down the line, Apache may sell Forties to another exploration and production (E&P) company. This is a key aspect of the oil industry ecosystem that's perhaps overshadowed by headline-grabbing mergers. Mature fields commonly get passed from the largest operators on down to successively smaller firms, who breathe new life into "tired" assets. It's not that the super majors are technologically backward or lazy. Given their market position, the incremental barrels just don't justify the more intensive effort required to recover them.

In nature, this would be called a detritus food chain. Smaller, more specialized organisms feed off of the scraps left behind by the big boys. This oil patch ecology is perfectly suited to what we see as the industry's key challenge in the decades ahead: squeezing extra oil out of the world's known accumulations. We'll assess ways of doing just that over the next three chapters.

Consider: *We have only consumed less than 8 percent (~1 Trillion barrels, Tb) of the world's identified reserves.*[87]

1010
1010
1010
1010

Chapter 9

Data Acquisition

Clean Score	Safety Score	Reliability Score	Affordability Score	X Degree Proven	X Likely Near-term Impact	TOTAL SCORE
15	10	12	25	100%	100%	62

The world's hydrocarbon resources, often referred to as original oil in place (OOIP) or original gas in place (OGIP), are tremendous, but economic, technological, and other constraints prevent operators from fully exploiting deposits. Worldwide recovery factors currently run around 35 percent at best.[88] (Some estimates even put the average recovery factor below 30 percent.[89]) There's a great deal of room for improvement there. And improvement will come.

A few years ago, an expert panel headed by Schlumberger veteran Tom Zimmerman projected that recovery factors from conventional wells will top 50 percent by 2030.[90] By far the biggest impact foreseen by the panel comes from increased wellbore-to-reservoir contact—in other words, drilling wells in greater proximity to where the oil sits. Geologists and engineers envision future well construction as analogous to a "vascular system where a complex network of veins and arteries provides an open pathway for blood flow to and from every part of the body."[91]

What technological advances will make this major increase in reservoir contact possible? Strikingly, it seems that nothing too revolutionary is required. The industry has been using measurement-while-drilling tools and steerable mud motors for decades. The key to future progress is advancing real-time data acquisition, which will help place the well bore with greater accuracy than has so far been possible.

As for the expected payoff, drilling consultant Tor Stein Olberg put it to the crowd at a 2009 conference this way: "If we can improve recovery rates by 20 per cent because we hit the target by within half a meter instead of five meters, there is immense potential to improve recovery."[92]

THE SEEING BIT

Traditionally, limited real-time information has been sent from tools residing in the wellbore up to operators at the surface by means of pulses transmitted through drilling mud. As of 2008, the industry standard for the speed of this communication system was three bits per second.[93]

At the time of its unveiling in 2008, Baker Hughes' aXcelerate service offered speeds seven times faster, but with such a heavy data stream required, these bit speeds of 20 times per second do not provide a game-changing improvement.[94] Precise real-time information will require data streams that are faster by many orders of magnitude.

So what if drillers transmitted the data via wires instead of mud? That's the idea behind wired drill pipe, which was proven several years ago but has yet to achieve rapid commercial uptake. In 2003, Grant Prideco's IntelliPipe system (funded in part by the DOE) achieved data rates of up to 2 million bits per second in a field test in Wyoming.[95] National Oilwell Varco has since sponged up this drill-pipe player, and markets the wired drill-pipe system, dubbed the IntelliServ Broadband Network, jointly with Schlumberger.

Today, IntelliServ only runs at the speed of an old 56.6k dial-up modem, so the broadband label remains somewhat aspirational. A current prototype, however, can transmit data at megabit speed, which would enable a technology called seismic-while-drilling (SWD).

With SWD, seismic returns in a fresh role, in which it relays accurate depth information in order to improve steering of the drill bit and identify hazards like pore pressure changes 1,000 feet ahead of the bit.

The way we currently drill for oil has been described by one Chevron engineer as driving with the headlights turned off at night.[96] SWD, in this modern implementation, would allow operators to "see" ahead of the bit like never before. Combined with the 4-D monitoring potential that we'll discuss in the next chapter, seismic's contribution to increasing recovery factors could potentially equal or surpass the mark it has made on exploration.

Imagine: We can extend our global current proven reserves from forty-two years (1.25 trillion barrels) to 56 years (1.66 trillion barrels) at current rates of use if oil recovery factors increase from 35 to 50 percent.[97]

Chapter 10

Enhanced Oil Recovery

Clean Score	Safety Score	Reliability Score	Affordability Score	X Degree Proven	X Likely Near-term Impact	TOTAL SCORE
25	0	25	25	100%	100%	75

F attening conventional recovery factors through better well design (among other important advances) is just the first step in getting more out of oil fields. Secondary recovery follows, in which a fluid (usually water) is injected to maintain reservoir pressure and to sweep extra oil out of the reservoir. Combined with extensive infill drilling, these injections are helping Norwegian national oil company Statoil to target a 66 percent oil recovery rate from its huge Statfjord field.[98] Of course, this is a definite outlier today, as the industry typically *leaves behind* two-thirds of the oil.[99]

After secondary recovery has concluded, a portion of the remaining oil may be subject to tertiary recovery, better known as enhanced oil recovery (EOR). With this technique, drillers still inject something into the reservoir, but now they're looking to change physical or chemical properties of the oil that's stubbornly resisting capture. There are three major forms of EOR: chemical flooding, gas flooding, and steam flooding. (Microbial EOR, a newer technique, isn't yet ready for prime time). A number of factors dictate which method is most appropriate, with oil depth and density being the key considerations.

PUTTING CARBON DIOXIDE TO WORK

Carbon dioxide EOR can bump overall recovery factors near 60 percent.[100] Denbury Resources, a world leader in this category, pursues a strategy of scooping up "depleted" fields and implementing CO_2 floods using naturally occurring carbon dioxide. The firm's Jackson Dome asset, located in Mississippi, is thought to be unique in the Gulf Coast area as a reservoir of trapped CO_2. Former owner Shell Oil did some early EOR work using Jackson Dome deposits in the 1980s, but the company sold the asset and a related CO_2 pipeline to an industrial gas supplier in 1996.[101] Denbury bought these same assets five years later for $42 million, shrewdly laying the frugal foundation for its soon-to-be multibillion dollar EOR empire.[102]

One of Denbury's greatest success stories is Mississippi's Mallalieu field, which the company bought for $4 million in 2001.[103] The asset had averaged 5,686 barrels per day at its peak,[104] but was producing just 75 barrels per day at the time of purchase.[105] Reversing this trend, Denbury had achieved positive net cash flow of $464 million from Mallalieu through the end of 2009.[106] Even considering other capital costs involved in the project, this was a staggering payoff.

In future EOR efforts, Denbury and other operators plan to use industrial sources of CO_2 once that market develops. If a slow transition away from oil is in the cards, squeezing out those incremental barrels will be important and valuable for society in the interim.

As for incremental or game-changing technological advances in this area, anything that could help to monitor and control the flood front as it sweeps through a reservoir would lead to significant improvements in yield. One promising area of DOE-sponsored research is the use of foams as mobility control agents.[107]

REAL-TIME SEISMIC

The growth of enhanced oil recovery depends greatly on continued improvements to monitoring systems. Seismic is still a good tool for the job, but getting to the next level will require seismic surveys to be ever more repeatable, cheap, and high signal-to-noise. The repeatability of the surveys is what carries seismic from 3-D to 4-D, adding the dimension of time by taking snapshots of the subsurface at regular intervals.

According to Olav Barkved, project manager for BP's Life of Field Seismic program, "If 4-D seismic can be done cheaply and frequently, it will have an enormous impact on the way that oil reservoirs are managed."[108]

One development bringing down cost (and thus allowing for greater frequency) is the introduction of fiber optic technology. In the late 1970s, the United States Navy started looking to develop hull-mounted fiber optic sensor arrays for submarine surveillance applications. Litton Industries won a subcontract to develop the prototype in the early 1990s and managed to meet all the Navy's demanding requirements for durability, sensitivity, etc.[109] As a result, these lightweight systems now grace the newest Virginia-class submarines.

But Litton didn't stop there. The company realized that its fiber optic sensors had major potential in enhanced oil recovery and began pursuing this opportunity. When Northrop Grumman purchased Litton in 2001, however, the defense giant considered EOR a non-core activity and abandoned the endeavor.

Some key Litton alumni have since gone off and formed a small company called US Sensor Systems. Now owned by Acorn Energy, the company has developed a geophone, based on the same fiber optic sensing technology, that is small, cheap, sensitive, and reliable. The device has performed in line with the DOE's "gold standard" conventional geophones at Lawrence Berkeley National Laboratory's facilities and is currently being field tested by a mid-sized independent oil exploration company.

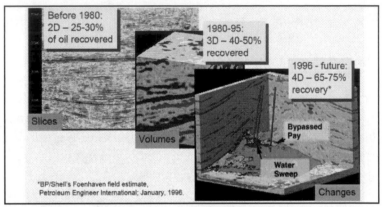

4-D Seismic Should Result in Significantly Enhanced Recovery Factors
Source: Petroleum Engineer International, January 1996

When installed as an array, the geophone's fiber optic sensors hold great promise for advanced down-hole seismic applications like CO_2 flood monitoring, but companies like Petroleo Brasileiro (Petrobras) have begun to embrace the technology for conventional reservoir monitoring, as well.[110] Fracture mapping is a third application, and we'll see the significance of that technique in the section on shale gas.

Down-hole 4-D seismic monitoring, also known as designer vertical seismic profiling (VSP), has great potential impact. The NETL recently endorsed this technology by saying, "America has over 218 billion barrels of known oil in shallow (less than 5,000 ft. subsurface) reservoirs—bypassed because it is uneconomic to extract with current technology—in thousands of aging oilfields. If developing technology such as microhole designer VSP could help unlock even 10 percent of that total, it would equal 10 years of OPEC imports at current rates."[111]

Dr. William F. Lawson, Director of the Strategic Center for Natural Gas & Oil, adds, "The barrier to 3-D VSP is cost, not technology. Yet the benefits are unarguable."[112]

Imagine: *"Enhanced Oil Recovery (EOR) has been used to optimize the production of less than 3 percent of the world's oil reserves".*[113]

In Situ Oil Sands Production

Clean Score	Safety Score	Reliability Score	Affordability Score	X Degree Proven	X Likely Near-term Impact	TOTAL SCORE
20	10	25	20	90%	100%	67.5

To date, most Canadian oil sands projects have involved a cavalcade of trucks with 13-foot tires hauling massive loads of oily muck out of open pits. These trucks take the mined material to a processing facility that extracts the bitumen and upgrades it to synthetic crude.

Because they're relatively heavy water users and greenhouse gas emitters, oil sands projects have become lightning rods for environmental groups. In recent years, in fact, Greenpeace activists have taken to chaining themselves to the giant dump trucks.

But only 20 percent of the oil sands are shallow enough to be excavated. The other 80 percent are only amenable to in situ recovery, which has the potential to deliver more acceptable environmental outcomes.[114] Even the Pembina Institute, a renewable energy think tank, has concluded that in situ projects, when applying industry best practices, could earn marks as high as 85 percent on the group's environmental scorecard.[115]

In situ recovery is a lot like conventional oil recovery, in that the oily, sandy mixture is retrieved through a wellbore. The bitumen requires some extra coaxing to flow to the surface, however. The predominant technique for doing so is called steam-assisted gravity drainage, or SAGD. This is a well-established commercial technology expected to out-produce oil sands mining by the middle of this decade.[116] Some of its most skilled practitioners are Cenovus Energy (a spin-off of Canadian gas giant Encana) and Suncor Energy, with Cenovus demonstrating a particular knack for lowering the steam-oil ratio, and thus the amount of water used to generate each barrel of oil.

The economics of SAGD projects also happen to be quite a bit better than those of mining projects. They offer staged growth, which spreads out capital costs over time. Furthermore, alternative processes like Petrobank's combustion-based non-steam "toe-to-heel air injection" (THAI) technique may one day surpass the productivity of SAGD.

Did You Know: In 2008 the Canadian oil sands represented half of that countries total crude production.[117]

```
1010
1010
1010
```
Chapter 12

Shale Fracturing

Clean Score	Safety Score	Reliability Score	Affordability Score	X Degree Proven	X Likely Near-term Impact	TOTAL SCORE
12	12	25	25	100%	100%	74

Shale gas seemingly arrived overnight circa 2008, when it became a front-page story in the nation's leading newspapers. As with most seemingly sudden developments, however, this one simmered in the background for many years before claiming public attention.

Attributing the breakout of shale gas recovery, Eric Potter of the University of Texas' Bureau of Economic Geology observed, "It wasn't high tech. It was persistence and experimentation on the part of one company that got this boom going."[118]

George Mitchell's eponymous E&P outfit, Mitchell Energy, was that one company. It began working on unlocking natural gas from the Barnett shale in the Dallas/Ft. Worth area in 1981. Mitchell's engineers had observed evidence of gas when drilling through the Barnett on the way to deeper formations, and executives began to wonder how to tap that gas. The low permeability of the rock didn't lend itself to conventional drilling methods. But by 1999, after 18 years of experimentation, Mitchell had figured out that hydraulic fracturing techniques—involving the high-pressure injection of a mix of water, sand, and chemicals—would make for consistently good wells.[119]

Hydraulic fracturing (or "fracking"), which is now used in nine out of ten natural gas wells in the United States,[120] was one key technology that enabled exploitation of the Barnett shale. The second big development was the advent of horizontal drilling, in which a drill bit heads down to the productive layer and then takes a 90-degree turn. This allows for a huge increase in contact with the laterally extensive hydrocarbon-bearing rock.

The arrival of steerable mud motors and measurement-while-drilling tools enabled the first serious development of horizontal drilling in the 1980s. That decade saw over 300 horizontal wells drilled.[121] In the 1990s, the number of horizontal wells increased by over 1,000 percent.[122]

Devon Energy bought out Mitchell Energy in 2001 for $3.5 billion, signaling the Barnett's move from the threshold of significance to the tipping point.[123] Horizontal drilling played a big part in that runaway growth. Devon, an early proponent, drilled nine horizontals in its 2002 program. Barnett players drilled a combined 130 horizontals the following year,[124] as total production went vertical:

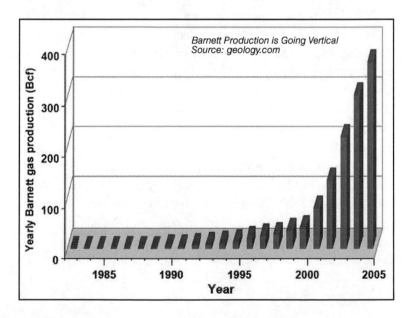

Today, in the third quarter of 2010, Devon alone expects to produce an all-time high of 1.2 billion cubic feet per day of natural gas from the Barnett shale.[125] This is a monster play, and it's not the only one. Following on the runaway success of the Barnett, independents began scouring North America for analogues. Southwestern Energy seized upon the Fayetteville Shale in Arkansas, picking up 343,000 acres for all of $11 million.[126] Range Resources was an early mover on the Marcellus Shale of Pennsylvania, and Chesapeake Energy unveiled the Haynesville Shale in northern Louisiana in 2008. These are huge gas deposits—so huge that most of the majors have either struck joint ventures with or (in the case of the ExxonMobil-XTO Energy merger) outright swallowed the early movers.

Shale gas is now going global. The hunt is on around the world for new unconventional plays, from South Africa to Sweden and from China to New Zealand. Few countries have anything remotely like the manpower, rigs, and other equipment needed to set off Barnett-sized gas booms of their own, however. Achieving production on the scale of the Barnett will take time.[127]

CRISIS AVERTED

Before shale gas, it looked as if we were going to become increasingly dependent on imported liquefied natural gas (LNG) to meet growing demand for this fuel. Books were published proclaiming "high noon" for natural gas and telling us that a natural gas crisis was a certainty within a matter of years.

But conventional wisdom changes as rapidly as new technology. The Massachusetts Institute of Technology concluded in a major new study that natural gas "will assume an increasing share of the U.S. energy mix over the next several decades, with the large unconventional resource playing a key role."[128]

The gas Cassandras have gone into retreat for the time being, though they're sure to be back one day, seeing all reservoirs as half-empty. Still, at this writing natural gas is so abundant that prices have become relatively depressed, and nearly all independents are racing to find "oily" plays to balance out their production profiles. Whether the target is primarily oil, "dry" gas, or liquids-rich "wet gas,"[129] all unconventional resource extraction will require new technologies from the service industry, and you can bet they'll come.

NEW METHODS REQUIRED

It's hard to drill a dry hole in these horizontally extensive plays, but proper well placement and "frac" design can make the difference between a profitable and an unprofitable field development program. For one thing, the tiny fractures being exploited present big challenges for standard reservoir-modeling software, as legacy modeling tools don't provide nearly high enough resolution at key points of contact.

This challenge neatly parallels the evolution from 2-D to 3-D imaging software that was met so brilliantly by Landmark Graphics decades ago. And, sure enough, co-founder John Mouton is again rising to the occasion. Mouton's new company, Object Reservoir, takes a page from the playbook of structural and aeronautical engineers by applying so-called finite element (FE) methods to reservoir modeling.

Finite element design has made huge strides in other manufacturing processes. If you're designing a car and modeling the impact of a head-on collision, for example, you don't need great precision in the rear of the car, but you require extremely high modeling precision near the point of impact. The same goes for airflow interacting with the wing of an aircraft. By allowing engineers to ignore elements that are irrelevant to the question they're trying to answer, finite element methods empower them to subject virtual wing models to virtual airflow instead of having to build and test a succession of physical models in wind tunnels. That breakthrough cuts design turnaround times from months to minutes.

Up until now, the shale gas players have gotten by on trial and error, which first consumed decades and still takes years. In much less time, FE methods will enable dynamic reservoir models to achieve resolutions down to fractions of an inch inside each frac. Mouton's new company looks poised both to reduce the cost and to accelerate the pace of advancement in these plays by moving experimentation from the field to the computer screen.

Expanding reserves: *Estimated U.S. natural gas reserves increased 35 percent from 2007 to 2009 according to the Potential Gas Committee, a panel made up of experts from the energy sector, academia and government estimated U.S. natural gas reserves at 2,074 trillion cubic feet. This is the highest estimate in the committee's 45-year history.*[130]

Chapter 13

The Digital Oilfield

Clean Score	Safety Score	Reliability Score	Affordability Score	X Degree Proven	X Likely Near-term Impact	TOTAL SCORE
25	15	25	25	100%	100%	100

Moore's Law famously posits that the number of transistors that can be inexpensively placed on a computer chip doubles every two years. [131] While there may be no Moore's Law of energy, there's also no question that the Information Technology revolution has driven the oil and gas sector to greater heights and will continue to do so. As it has in the past three decades, data will lie at the heart of this ongoing transformation.

The so-called digital oil field, according to Chris Reddick, Vice President of E&P Technology for BP, "represents the biggest opportunity to change the way we manage our facilities, wells and reservoirs that we have seen in the past 30 years."[132]

The digital oilfield is highly instrumented and highly automated. Its rewards, if implemented broadly, are massive. The analysts at IHS Cambridge Energy Research Associates project that the digital oilfield can unlock 125 billion barrels of incremental oil reserves, raise production rates by as much as 10 percent, and slash operating costs by up to 25 percent.[133]

The advances we've described in real-time acquisition and modeling are important but hardly sufficient to bring us the "digital oilfield of the future" that the industry began embracing strongly over the past decade. Organizing the data so that it's accessible and useful is a real challenge, just as it was in the transition to 3-D seismic.

An SPE Digital Energy survey of upstream engineers found that 91 percent of respondents spent more than half of their time hunting for, formatting, and preparing data for analysis. Fifty-five percent had less than a quarter of their professional time available to actually analyze the data and form actionable decisions.[134]

The industry can do a much better job of getting data out of silos and into the hands of its knowledge workers. One key step is to achieve standard formatting across the industry, and the Energistics consortium is making good strides in this area by publishing open, non-proprietary standards.[135] As far as software platforms go, operators want to be able to cherry–pick among the industry's best offerings, rather than be stuck with one vendor. "Middleware" like OpenSpirit makes that cross-vendor integration possible.

Better software will enable automation and remote support, both of which are key to getting more out of the fields, as well as from an overstretched workforce. BP has reported that mining two years of pressure and temperature data from its fields with new computer technology gives the firm insights that formerly would have taken up to 15 years to glean.[136] These insights can then be used to predict results before a drill bit breaks the ground.

Predictive analytics are just one realm in which the upstream business can take a cue from the refining folks. Refineries already sport a lot of the features that will likely be integrated into the digital oil field of the future. They're highly instrumented and automated. Predictive maintenance, pioneered by process control specialists like Emerson Electric, prevents outages and accidents before they happen.[137]

Refineries have also adopted wireless transmitters, creating self-organizing mesh networks of devices in communication with one another.[138] With chips in every dumb device, this network becomes very intelligent.

If you want a preview of the digital oil field, look to the digital refinery.

Imagine: 125 billion barrels of "unlocked" domestic oil reserves would power all U.S. oil needs at the current rate of consumption of 7 million barrels per day for an additional 50 years.[139]

NATIONAL PRIORITY
Getting More from Coal

I n 2008, the United States derived around 23 percent of its primary energy supply from coal.[140] That doesn't quite get to the heart of how big a role coal plays in our lives, though. When you narrow the focus to electric power, coal dominates the picture, at close to 50 percent of net generation:[141]

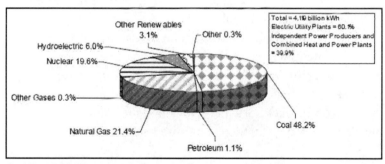

Coal-Fired Power Dominates Our Electricity Supply
Source: Energy Information Administration, Annual Energy Review, 2009

Annual coal consumption amounts to roughly 7,500 pounds per American,[142] which is about the weight of a female African elephant.[143]

The concerns regarding coal are obviously quite different from those surrounding oil. Coal is abundant and affordable. No one feels anxious about all the "easy coal" disappearing, because that's nowhere near to being the case. And, as we'll see, coal extraction technology has become incredibly efficient.

The primary problem with coal is the host of negative environmental consequences that result from its extraction and, especially, combustion. As regulations tighten, the cost of new coal-fired generation increasingly reflects these externalities. And well-organized opposition to new coal plants ties most of them up in the courts, further increasing costs and uncertainty.

Utilities can still get the occasional new coal unit built, often through an agreement to retrofit or retire older units and perhaps sweeten the pot with some renewables. The willingness of utilities to make these concessions shows how determined they are to maintain supplies of reliable power. No utility CEO wants to preside over the next major blackout or brownout. Notwithstanding their efforts, if and when such an event occurs one might expect that the obstacles to building new coal-fired power plants will ease considerably.

The authors realize it borders on heresy in some circles to argue that new coal plants should be a part of the nation's future energy mix. But argue this position we must. Because the fact remains that—built to exacting standards and coupled with retirement of the oldest, least efficient, and most polluting units— the construction of modern coal-fired generators offers a net gain for society.

The industry has developed ways of dramatically cutting pollutants like sulfur oxides, nitrogen oxide, and mercury at an acceptable cost. Carbon dioxide is a different challenge entirely, and we'll discuss that issue separately.

Chapter 14

Smart Mines

Clean Score	Safety Score	Reliability Score	Affordability Score	X Degree Proven	X Likely Near-term Impact	TOTAL SCORE
20	25	25	25	90%	90%	85.5

Since 1950, coal mining productivity as measured by short tons per employee-hour is up roughly eightfold in the United States.[144] In that time, the number of coal miners has dropped by approximately 350,000, and fatalities are also down sharply.[145]

Underground mining, predominant in the eastern part of the country, has partially shifted from the conventional room-and-pillar method, which would once leave over half a coal seam behind in pillars supporting the mine shaft, to longwall extraction, which is heavily mechanized and uses self-advancing hydraulic ceiling supports.

A key enabling technology for the longwall method was the all-electric shearing machine, first introduced by Joy Mining Machinery in the mid-1970s.[146] Shearing machines proceed along a coalface, cutting coal at rates pushing 2,700 tons per hour (or three-quarters of a ton per second).[147] One-hundred-fifty men can now produce over six times the output that 1,200 men could achieve before the introduction of the shearer.[148]

According to *Coal Age*, there are 44 longwall mines in the country.[149] They're clearly very efficient, but the deadly explosion at Massey Energy's West Virginia Upper Big Branch mine in April 2010 demonstrates that safety issues have not been fully resolved. Methane sensors, fiber optic data transmission, and two-way communications have all made contributions to worker safety, but most underground mines have not met the government's requirements for new communications and tracking gear. Only around eight percent of facilities had these systems fully operational as of March 2010, according to the U.S. Mine Safety and Health Administration.[150]

There is a major opportunity today to improve the cost, performance, and reliability of these underground safety systems. Following a successful trial under contract with the National Institute for Occupational Safety and Health, US Sensor Systems is working on commercializing an all-optical system to provide both real-time miner tracking and two-way emergency communications.

WESTERN WONDERS

The productivity of surface mines west of the Mississippi is pretty stunning. In 2008, 1,458 total U.S. mines produced 1.17 billion short tons of coal. The 17 surface mines located in Wyoming's Powder River Basin (PRB) produced 42 percent of all that coal.[151] Arch Coal's Black Thunder complex alone supplies over ten percent of the nation's coal annually.[152]

Key enablers of this enormous productivity are giant draglines and electric shovels. At first glance these seem to be no more than economies of scale at work. Hidden behind or within the hardware, however, are essential software systems such as QNX Software Systems' Neutrino RTOS. This embedded operating system makes drills and shovels smart, providing the equipment (and its skilled operator) with critical positioning and terrain data in real time.[153] The software leverages economies of connection.

Did You Know: *There is estimated to be enough minable coal in the United States to supply all of North America's energy needs for 200 years at current rates of usage.*[154]

Chapter 15

Reengineering the Coal Plant

Clean Score	Safety Score	Reliability Score	Affordability Score	X Degree Proven	X Likely Near-term Impact	TOTAL SCORE
25	25	25	25	100%	50%	50

The United States accounts for over half of all coal plants over the age of 30 in the world.[155] Whereas the vast majority of China's coal-fired capacity has been installed since 1985, most of our installed capacity came online before 1985.[156] The vintage of our plants helps to make clear why average thermal efficiencies have flatlined at 32 or 33 percent for decades.[157]

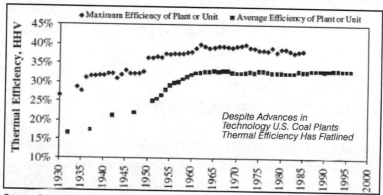

Source: International Energy Agency, "The Economics of Transition in the Power Sector", January 2010

83

One explanation of this state of affairs is the fact that life extensions for existing units have proven far more economical than retirements and replacements. According to the Clean Air Act, older plants were supposed to see modern environmental controls installed as part of any significant refurbishment, but things have played out differently. Some blame the utilities for slipping major upgrades through the net under the guise of "repairs." Others point to the regulators, who have effectively prevented utilities from making efficiency improvements that would have a beneficial emissions impact. Ironically, environmental groups have also impeded progress in fleet efficiency by blocking the construction of modern units.

Parcel out the blame however you like. The bottom line has been stagnation: power generators continuing to run inefficient plants when the technology exists to do better.

The merits to retiring the oldest coal-fired units should be clear enough to everyone. The European Union, Canada and China have all recently taken steps to phase out older, dirtier units.[158] The U.S. must certainly follow, and as we look to replace this significant chunk of generating capacity over the next two decades or so, the big challenge will be to supply reliable and affordable power with a reduced environmental impact.

Let's take a look at what new coal-fired units bring to the table.

SUPERSEDING THE SUBCRITICAL

Central to a coal-fired unit's efficiency is the boiler, which creates the steam that turns the turbine that generates the electricity. Typical plants have "subcritical" boilers that operate at 1800 to 2,400 pounds per square inch (psi) of pressure.[159] Supercritical boilers—which actually skip the boiling part—operate at pressures above 3200 psi and at much higher temperatures.[160] This leads to significant thermodynamic efficiency gains.

Supercritical plants were popular in the U.S. in the early 1970s, but the steel didn't hold up well under extreme pressure and temperature conditions. As a result, we largely abandoned this approach, while Europe and Asia continued to pursue it. But supercritical plants are coming back (if we let them). MidAmerican Energy's Walter Scott Jr. Energy Center Unit 4, dubbed Plant of the Year in 2007, was the first new supercritical unit built in the U.S. in 16 years.[161]

American Electric Power is looking to take things a step further with its planned ultra-supercritical Turk plant in Arkansas. Turk's spec sheet suggests a thermal efficiency of about 39 percent, which may understate its potential.[162] China Huaneng Group's Yuhuan plant, powered by four 1,000-megawatt (MW) Mitsubishi ultra-supercritical boilers, runs at a reported 45 percent efficiency.[163]

In any case, it is clear that ultra-supercritical plants are at least 35 percent more efficient than our current fleet. That means 35 percent less coal burned for the same electrical output, and a comparable reduction in toxics released into the environment.[164]

Another route to higher efficiency from new coal plants is gasification. The integrated gasification combined cycle (IGCC) process turns coal into a synthetic gas, removes impurities, and then burns the gas.

Capital costs for IGCC are uncomfortably high today, but have not deterred all utilities. Southern Company currently hopes to build a 582 MW IGCC plant in Mississippi for $2.88 billion.[165] Duke Energy projects the same cost for its 618 MW Edwardsport IGCC project in Indiana.[166]

One way to drive down the cost of IGCC is to move manufacturing to China, which is the approach being taken by Mitsubishi.[167] More dramatic cost savings resulting from technological innovation will need to emerge soon for IGCC to represent a compelling alternative to supercritical plants in the next decade.

REBUILDING THE FLEET

The economic downturn has bought the utility sector some time. Power demand is down, which takes the edge off of capacity constraints. Once the economy recovers, however, the industry will get right back to worrying about our nation's electric generation capacity. The necessary retirement of units that can't justify the cost of environmental controls will compound this issue.

New power generation plants must be built to satisfy demand from a growing economy, and new coal-fired units offering significant reductions in coal usage and emissions deserve to be part of the mix. But for new supercritical or IGCC units to be competitive with natural gas, nuclear, wind, and other renewables, the industry will need to drive down the cost of pollution controls and carbon capture and storage solutions. We'll spend the balance of this section looking at these two areas.

Imagine: China is seeking to decrease its energy intensity from coal-fired power plants by 20 percent by upgrading their plants with supercritical boilers.[168]

Chapter 16

Cleaning Up Combustion

Clean Score	Safety Score	Reliability Score	Affordability Score	X Degree Proven	X Likely Near-term Impact	TOTAL SCORE
25	20	25	20	100%	100%	90

oal combustion produces emissions that are linked to negative respiratory, cardiovascular, and neurological effects. These pollutants include particulate matter, nitrogen oxides (NO_x), sulfur oxides (SO_x), and mercury.

As a result of EPA regulations beginning with the Clean Air Act of 1970, emissions of key "criteria pollutants" have fallen significantly. Through 2008, aggregate emissions from all six criteria pollutants fell by 60 percent since 1970, by 54 percent since 1980 and by 41 percent since 1990.[169] Not only have power generators made good progress in response to these mandates, there's plenty of room for further reductions.

The EPA introduced a new 1-hour SO_2 standard in June 2010 and undoubtedly will continue to tighten its standards.[170] We can also expect eventual federal restrictions on mercury, which is a potent neurotoxin. For now, states like Michigan are taking mercury regulation into their own hands.[171]

Compliance doesn't come cheap, of course. About 16 per-

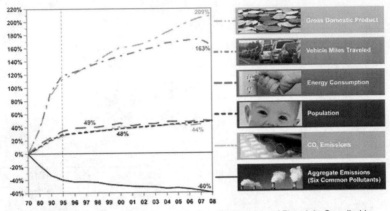

Regulated Emissions are Down Substantially Despite Doubling of Electricity Supplied by Coal-Fired Plants Source: U.S. Department of Environmental Protection, Airtrends 2009

cent of the costs for Integrys Energy Group's new Weston 4 unit in Wisconsin went for air pollution controls.[172] Duke Energy attributes roughly 40 percent of the cost of its Cliffside project in Cleveland to emissions controls.[173] Any technology that can make pollution control cheaper or more effective is a huge winner for everyone.

PURGING PARTICULATES AND SCRUBBING SO_x

Thanks to the installation of electrostatic precipitators (ESPs) and fabric filters, either of which can very effectively capture fly ash, particulate (PM_{10}) emissions from coal-fired plants dropped 89 percent from 1.68 million tons in 1970 to 0.188 million tons in 2005.[174] To some extent these efforts become victims of their own success, however, as the worthy goal of continuing reductions requires increasingly complex and costly solutions.

The prime SO_x reduction tool is the flue gas desulfurization (FGD) unit, commonly known as a scrubber. With this technique, the "flue gas" exhaust passes through a limestone slurry, which captures the SO_2. The resulting calcium sulfite can then be oxidized to create gypsum, a component of wallboard and cement. These "wet" scrubbers achieve SO_2 reductions of up to 99 percent.[175]

As of 2008, 140.3 gigawatts (GW) of coal-fired capacity, or around 42 percent of national nameplate generating capacity, had scrubbers installed.[176] That year saw the biggest increase in scrubber installations since 1995,[177] so the industry appears to have picked up the pace of retrofits. Or at least it had, prior to the recession throwing a wrench into utility capital budgets.

Scrubbers are very expensive on account of all the pumps, valves, and other heavy-duty equipment involved. (One pump could fill an Olympic swimming pool in under ten minutes.)[178] Fully loaded capital costs came in at $370 per kilowatt in a recent survey,[179] which translates to $185 million for a 500 MW plant. Furthermore, wet FGDs typically consume 2–3 percent of a plant's gross electrical output.[180]

"Dry" scrubbers offer lower capital costs and smaller footprints, but they traditionally haven't operated as efficiently, and they also create a larger solid waste stream. MidAmerican Energy's new 800 MW supercritical unit in Iowa, named Power Plant of the Year in 2007, makes use of a series of three dry scrubbers.[181] These units appear to be making some inroads, but wet scrubbers are still the most common.

KNOCKING OUT NO$_x$

The traditional approach to reducing nitrogen oxide emissions is through combustion controls like low-NO$_x$ burners and over-fired air. These primary measures are the most cost-effective, and can deliver over 50 percent NO$_x$ removal efficiency.[182] But even that's not sufficient to meet today's increasingly stringent standards.

A more thorough method of NOx control is called selective catalytic reduction (SCR). SCR systems inject ammonia into the post-combustion exhaust or "flue gas" stream, breaking down the NOx into nitrogen and water in the presence of a catalyst. Emissions reductions from the SCR unit alone generally fall in the 80 to 90 percent range.[183]

In 1997, there were only six SCR-equipped coal-fired units in the United States, representing less than 2 GW of generation capacity.[184] Today, over 100 GW of coal-fired capacity have been outfitted with SCR systems,[185] so they're not far behind scrubbers in terms of deployment.

The cost of an SCR runs from $118 to $150 per kilowatt, or around $65.5 million for a 500 MW plant.[186] An added expense comes from the need to replace the catalyst (which is usually vanadium-based), which can get plugged up with fly ash. The new Clean Air Interstate Rule require operators to run their SCRs year-round, as opposed to just five months previously, which should at least double the frequency of catalyst replacement.

CoaLogix, a North Carolina–based firm owned by Acorn Energy, leads the market in catalyst management and regeneration. The company estimates that these combined services can save a utility 70 to 80 percent of its catalyst costs.[187] Since there is roughly $1.5 billion worth of catalyst installed in North America, companies like CoaLogix have a major opportunity to reduce the cost of pollution control. As a bonus, the recycling of catalyst keeps many tons of waste out of landfills. CoaLogix estimates that within several years the regeneration of catalyst will provide the equivalent annual offset of CO_2 as that of replacing 100,000 conventional gas cars with electric vehicles.

Another avenue for lowering the expense of NO_x reduction is the use of a non-catalytic reduction (SNCR) system, either alone or in conjunction with a smaller SCR. Two such offerings are from FuelTek[203] and Nalco Mobotec[204] claims lower NO_x reductions at 30 to 70 percent of the cost of a conventional SCR. For now, SCRs dominate the market for major NO_x removal, especially in large units.

MUZZLING MERCURY

Mercury controls are a new development, as no federal rule yet requires them. Some plants have installed systems in anticipation of future regulation but won't use them until the law demands it.

If properly configured, existing controls (SCRs, FGDs, and particle control devices) can take out a high percentage of the mercury, depending on the composition of the coal. In many cases, though, plants will need new equipment to attain likely goals.

The best-developed technology is sorbent injection, which blows a powder (usually activated carbon) into the flue gas stream to bind with the mercury. A fabric filter, or "baghouse," then catches the resulting particulates.[188]

Activated carbon is an expensive process that can cost a plant $1 to $10 million per year.[189] In a search for more economical alternatives, the DOE has developed a so-called Thief Process that uses partially burned coal in place of activated carbon.[190] Other novel approaches, such as Alstom's KNX technology, seek to oxidize the mercury by adding a halogen like chlorine or bromine, making the mercury easier to remove with existing controls. This technology has already been commercialized in the waste incineration sector and appears to offer a strong option for units burning Wyoming coal.[191]

We haven't talked about the impact of I.T. in this chapter, but it's well worth mentioning that many of the aforementioned solutions wouldn't be possible without the extensive use of computational fluid dynamics modeling and simulation software. In many ways, cleaner coal comes to you via computing power.

Consider: *One-third of the capital cost of a coal-fired power plant today are the air pollution control systems. According to the McIlvaine Company the number of air pollution control* *systems on coal-fired power plants is going to increase dramatically in the next ten years. FGDs will increase from 650 units in 2010 to 1100 in 2020 and SCRs will increase from 490 in 2010 to 1000 in 2020. Likewise, SNCR units are expected to grow from 210 units to 445 .*[192]

Chapter 17

Carbon Capture and Sequestration

Clean Score	Safety Score	Reliability Score	Affordability Score	X Degree Proven	X Likely Near-term Impact	TOTAL SCORE
15	0	0	0	0	0	0

I f there's a deal-breaker for coal, it's not the mining accidents or the mercury, but carbon dioxide. Coal emits nearly twice as many pounds of CO_2 per million BTU as natural gas,[193] and coal plants account for 81 percent of CO_2 emissions from the electric power sector.[194]

In 2007, the Supreme Court found that greenhouse gases (GHGs) fit within the Clean Air Act definition of air pollutants. The EPA followed in 2009 with an "endangerment finding" that paves the way for regulation of GHGs, including carbon dioxide.[195]

As of July 2010, atmospheric carbon dioxide levels weighed in at a seasonally adjusted 390 parts per million, or 0.039 percent of the earth's atmosphere.[196] Scientists warned a few years ago that we risk catastrophic climate change over the next century if we exceed concentrations of 0.055 percent. That shifted to 0.045 percent, and now some experts say we need to cut back to 0.035 percent.[197]

Although some people continue to express disagreement with the notion of man-made climate change, general consensus has clearly put carbon in the crosshairs. If the Senate doesn't legislate a carbon reduction scheme, the EPA probably will regulate one.

Meanwhile, the uncertainty surrounding what the government will or won't do to address this issue hovers over the calculations any utility might make. Until a regulatory regime settles into place, most managers who are considering new coal plants will likely sit on their hands.

BURN IT AND BURY IT

Arguably the only way to retain coal-fired power plants under an aggressive carbon-cutting regime (President Obama campaigned on an 80 percent reduction of GHGs by 2050)[198] is to capture the CO_2 and stash it underground. The energy requirements, cost, and scale of such an undertaking, however, would be staggering.[199]

First of all, carbon capture and sequestration (CCS) takes a lot of energy itself. Advanced Resources International recently modeled a 25 percent parasitic load for retrofits capturing 90 percent of the CO_2 that a coal plant emits.[200] That means you only get 375 megawatts out of your 500 MW plant—the rest of the energy going to carbon sequestration. Applied across half of the existing coal fleet—roughly 157 gigawatts of net capacity[201]—that's over 39 GW of generation capacity being diverted to CCS, an amount that exceeds the total electric generation capacity in all but five U.S. states.[202]

In addition to this drain on production, capital costs for CCS will be considerable. At Scottish and Southern Energy's Ferrybridge Station in Yorkshire, England, the carbon capture cost of a planned retrofit has been pegged at around $200 million.[203] Measured in cents per kilowatt-hour, CCS retrofits and rebuilds would at least triple the total cost of energy coming out of a coal plant, according to MIT.[204]

But the storage aspect of this scheme is perhaps the most daunting of all. A one-gigawatt coal plant emits a volume of CO_2 that, if liquefied, equals about 100,000 barrels per day by volume.[205] That's equivalent to daily crude oil production in the state of Kansas, which is ranked ninth in the country.[206]

By 2030, if the President's goals are met, the nation would be capturing and storing over 1 billion tons of carbon emissions from electric generating units annually.[207] Statoil's North Sea Sleipner natural gas project, the first to commercialize CO_2 storage in a deep saline aquifer, sequesters about 1 million tons per year.[208] Using that method, utilities would thus need to construct the equivalent of 1,000 Sleipners at existing coal plants within 20 years to meet the stated goals.

Carbon capture for enhanced oil recovery can take some of the pressure off of this storage challenge. So can cement plants using CO_2 as an input, as startup Calera seeks to do.[209] In this sense they're emulating companies like Headwaters, which turns coal combustion by-products like fly ash into valuable products. The enormous scale of CO_2 emissions, however, suggests that the only realistic course would be to stick most of the captured carbon in the ground.

If we decide that slashing our carbon emissions is the least regrettable pathway to follow in the face of possible climate change, it's hard to see coal-fired electric plants competing with those fed by other fuels. In that case, coal's competitiveness as a major power source may in effect be legislated away. That leaves natural gas and nuclear power as the clearest near-term and long-term successors to coal in a carbon-capped world.

Think: From 1990 to 2007, the per capita emissions of CO_2 in the United States fell by 1.8 percent. During that same period the per capita CO_2 emissions in China increased 132 percent[210]

NATIONAL PRIORITY
Getting More from Nuclear

uclear power satisfies more than 75 percent of France's electricity needs.[211] In the United States, it provides roughly 20 percent.[212] Still, the U.S. is the largest nuclear power producer in the world, at roughly double France's output.[213] And anyone who thinks the industry has been dormant since the 1979 Three Mile Island incident has missed an important story.

Nuclear power sits at an interesting crossroads right now. On the one hand, there are signs of a renaissance. Largely on account of its zero-carbon emissions profile, nuclear has found new champions, ranging from Microsoft's Bill Gates to Greenpeace co-founder Patrick Moore and Gaia hypothesizer James Lovelock. Secretary of Energy Stephen Chu, who holds a Nobel Prize in Physics, says unequivocally: "If we are serious about cutting carbon pollution then nuclear power must be part of the solution."[214] Southern Company has heard the call. It accepted an $8.3 billion federal loan guarantee for its two new units at Plant Vogtle near Waynesboro, Georgia, and more guarantees are expected soon.[215]

On the other hand, plenty of concerns and anxieties remain. The federal government has taken Yucca Mountain off the table as a potential long-term storage location for nuclear waste. The Vermont Senate has voted to block a license extension for the state's early-vintage Yankee Nuclear Power Station, following the discovery of leaked radioactive tritium and other problems at the site.[216] And risks of proliferation pose perennial global security worries.

Patrick Moore says that safety and waste are the two main concerns surrounding nuclear.[217] That may be true for existing plants, but if the nation allows them to be built, the next generation of nuclear facilities could well be different.

In its study *America's Energy Future: Technology and Transformation*, the National Research Council suggests that barriers to further nuclear deployment "can be reduced or eliminated if the first handful of [new] plants are constructed on schedule and on budget, and they demonstrate initial safe and secure operation."[218]

That quote hits upon the authors' primary concern with nuclear: getting new plants built on time and on budget, with a minimum of "teething problems." While we'll highlight some innovative new reactor designs below, we're going to focus just as much on mega-project management, which could be the key to sustaining the nuclear renaissance. After all, given the complexity of nuclear plants and a necessarily stringent regulatory regime, project management is the biggest pain point in this industry and therefore where the biggest opportunity for improvement lies today.

Chapter 18

Cranking Up Capacity

Clean Score	Safety Score	Reliability Score	Affordability Score	X Degree Proven	X Likely Near-term Impact	TOTAL SCORE
25	25	25	25	100%	100%	100

ssuance of construction permits and operating licenses for nuclear power units peaked in 1974, five years before Three Mile Island.[219] Many factors weighed on nuclear construction prior to the accident, not least of which was the sky-high rate of inflation at the time. But Three Mile Island was the nail in the coffin, bringing a halt to new reactor orders.

Despite the freeze—with all 41 reactor orders placed after 1973 eventually cancelled[220]—total operable units actually continued to rise until 1990, when the number of reactors topped out at 112.[221] In that year, electric output from nuclear plants rested at nearly double the level of 1980, as both the number of units and capacity factors increased.[222]

A capacity factor measures a plant's output relative to its total capacity. By 1990, this measure had reached 66 percent fleet-wide. In 2002, the industry exceeded 90 percent for the first time. As a result, while total operable capacity declined slightly, nuclear output expanded by 35 percent.[223]

Several things drove this growth from within.

One path to increased capacity utilization is to spend more time running a nuclear unit, and less time refueling it. Thanks to new fuel designs, which permit better "burnup," many plants have now extended their fuel cycle from 12 months to 18–24 months.[224] Operators have also become more efficient in the refueling process, significantly slashing average refueling outage days:

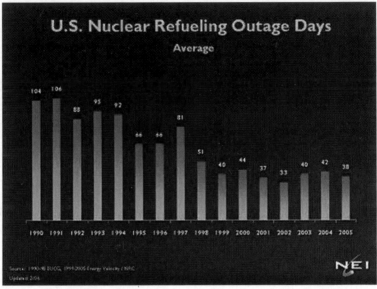

U.S. Nuclear Refueling Outage Days
Source: Energy Velocity/Nuclear Regulatory Commission/Nuclear Energy Institute

The second key factor has been the implementation of capacity upgrades ("uprates" in industry parlance), which have added the equivalent of over five new reactors without breaking any new ground.[225]

Uprates range from below two percent to as much as 20 percent of added capacity, depending on the extent of the modifications.[226] Shaw Group is one of the leaders in this area, having participated in around half of all uprate projects in this country.[227] The company reported in early 2010 that it's chasing 60 or

70 additional projects, and that they're getting bigger.[228] Exelon alone seeks 1,300 to 1,500 MW in uprates by 2017.[229]

Thus, much like improvements in the oil refining industry, which has also added capacity by tweaking existing plants, the nation's nuclear power infrastructure has grown without increasing its footprint.

The folks at EXCEL Services, a leading nuclear consultancy, make a strong case for crediting some of the gains in nuclear productivity to an initiative called Improved Technical Specifications (ITS). Nearly three-quarters of America's nuclear reactors (76 of 104) have undergone ITS conversions, and EXCEL worked on every single one of them.[230]

Standard technical specifications are essentially industry best practices that the Nuclear Regulatory Commission (NRC) publishes for each reactor design (General Electric, Westinghouse, etc.).[231] Standardization across the fleet improves communication and knowledge sharing both among operators and between operators and regulators. Improved specifications were issued in the early 1990s, primarily to improve safety. A safer plant is more reliable, more productive, and more profitable. How much more profitable? Full ITS conversion currently pays back its investment within two to three years, making it an easy sell.[232]

EXTENDED LIFE

While further efficiency gains remain to be squeezed out of the nuclear reactor fleet, the bigger issue in coming years will be ensuring that older reactors can continue to operate safely well beyond their 30- or 40-year design lives.

One way to extend reactor longevity is through advanced modeling and simulation. With a virtual reactor, engineers can study the interaction of complex phenomena and optimize the fleet based on the results of that simulation activity.

The DOE-sponsored Consortium for Advanced Simulation of Light Water Reactors is taking this exact approach. Part of the new Nuclear Energy Modeling and Simulation Hub, this is a public-private partnership comprising four government labs, three universities, and three energy companies.[233] The consortium employs three of the fastest supercomputers in the world in its quest to make reactors stronger for longer.[234]

Consider: *Total electrical capacity from U.S. nuclear power plants has grown by 800 percent since 1970*.[235]

Chapter 19

Mega-Project
Management

Clean Score	Safety Score	Reliability Score	Affordability Score	X Degree Proven	X Likely Near-term Impact	TOTAL SCORE
20	25	25	25	90%	100%	85.5

At the end of 2003, France's Areva won a contract to build the world's first European Pressurized Reactor (EPR) in Finland. The EPR is one of eight major new Generation III/III+ reactor models being introduced around the world, all of which offer more standardized designs, longer planned operating lives (generally 60 years), and other improvements over the prior generation.[236]

Areva originally planned to complete the Olkiluoto 3 (OL3) reactor in 2009 at a cost of €3 billion. After experiencing a host of construction problems, however, the company has now taken €2.7 billion in provisions for cost overruns, nearly doubling the projected cost and adding at least three years to its original timetable.[237]

This sort of construction management failure is exactly what the nuclear industry needs to avoid, yet it comes in spite of the fact that Areva has an excellent reputation as a nuclear designer and vendor. Notably, however, this is the first time the company has struck off on its own to construct a reactor.

One cheeky rule of thumb in the nuclear EPC (engineering, procurement, and construction) industry is that a pound of steel equals a pound of documents. Since a plant's reactor containment buildings can be comprised of over 100 million pounds of steel reinforcing bars, the quip is a bit of an exaggeration.[238] Still, the construction of a nuclear plant really does require about a million documents or more.[239] And the paperwork doesn't stop there. One consultant's study found that a nuclear plant creates 40 million documents across its complete life cycle.[240] Although that study was produced in 1979, there is little reason to believe the numbers have improved with time.

Document management is just one aspect of a comprehensive project information control system. Another is the management of vendor deliverables, and a third is workflow management. This all sounds like corporate gobbledygook, but effective processes for handling data and knowledge throughout the multi-year licensing, construction, and certification of a plant, could potentially prevent billions of dollars in cost overruns.

Given the stakes with regard to money and safety, project intelligence can mean the difference between nuclear rebirth and nuclear stillbirth. Acorn Energy's Coreworx subsidiary is one of the companies working to ensure the former outcome.

Coreworx customers currently deploy its enterprise software platform across over 500 large capital projects in the oil & gas, power generation, and mining sectors. The company counts Chevron and Fluor among its anchor customers, the latter company being one of the biggest EPC firms in the world. For example, Toshiba hired Fluor in 2007 to provide engineering, procurement and construction-related services to support its construction of two new reactors at NRG Energy's South Texas Project Nuclear Generating Station in Bay City.[241]

Coreworx's latest offering is the industry's first complete solution for ITAAC—or inspection, test and analysis acceptance criteria.[242] ITAAC verifies that a facility has been constructed according to specifications in the combined licenses and that everything will function as advertised. The operator can't load nuclear fuel until it has met all the ITAAC criteria, which is a substantial endeavor. [243] A nuclear facility consisting of two AP1000 reactors, for example, has almost 2000 ITAAC requirements consisting of some 60,000 deliverables and millions of supporting documents.[244] If the ITAAC closure was spread evenly over the final 30 months of the project it would represent about one deliverable every 20 minutes, 24/7.

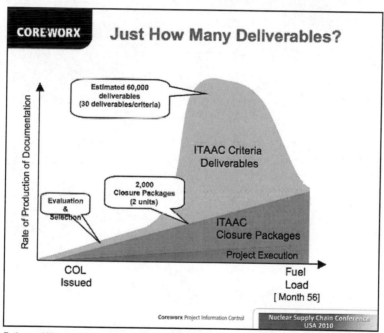

Estimated Number of Documents Required to Start Up a Nuclear Power Plant Under a Combined Operating License
Source: Coreworx presentation, Nuclear Supply Chain Conference, USA 2010

Nuclear power stations are marvels of science and engineering, but their future viability may rely more on computer science than nuclear physics. Companies like Coreworx are bringing the power of Information Technology to bear at the important early stages of the nuclear renaissance.

Did You Know: In the United States, the federal government provides subsidies equivalent to $30 per megawatt-hour of capacity for refined coal, $24.34 for solar and $23.37 for wind. Compare that to its subsidy for nuclear: just $1.59 per megawatt-hour of capacity.[245]

Chapter **20**

Modularity

Clean Score	Safety Score	Reliability Score	Affordability Score	X Degree Proven	X Likely Near-term Impact	TOTAL SCORE
25	25	25	25	90%	75%	67.5

n parallel with the development of new, large-scale re-actors like the EPR, another type of reactor design is emerging: the Small Modular Reactor (SMR).

Energy Secretary Chu detailed some of the benefits of SMRs in a *Wall Street Journal* op-ed in March 2010:

- Compact design, affording factory assembly and transportation by truck or rail
- Suitable for locations without capacity for a large-scale plant
- Reduced capital costs and construction times
- Little or no water use
- Potential to burn used fuel or nuclear waste[246]

If the industry doesn't embrace mega-project management and reap its rewards, or if financing of big plants just proves too onerous, modular facilities may save the day.

The smallest of the SMRs is Toshiba's 10-megawatt 4S (for Super-Safe, Small, and Simple) reactor.[247] On the other end of the spectrum, GE Hitachi Nuclear Energy's Generation IV PRISM (for Power Reactor Innovative Small Module) technology promises 311 MW of electrical output.[248] The enormous range in output between these two models demonstrates the flexibility that this technology can provide.

Designed to produce 125 MW of power, Babcock & Wilcox's mPower reactor leverages modularity to emphasize the nuclear power station's potential as a direct replacement for old coal-fired plants.[249] Rather than purchasing a single reactor, if desired an operator can order up a "two-pack" or "four-pack" of these units for 250 MW or 500 MW of capacity, respectively. These configurations match the general capacity range of large, older coal plants. [250]

The key challenge for SMRs will be to get a few of these novel designs certified while the window of opportunity remains wide open. Bernstein Research estimates that 12 percent of coal-fired plants will be retired in the next decade.[251] B&W expects the first mPower reactor to go online by 2018 at the earliest.[252] If these units aren't available within a year or two of that goal, they could miss a key period of coal plant retirements.

The timing is tight, but cooperative efforts between the public and private sectors (perhaps including the military) may bring one or two SMRs into service before 2020.

Interesting Fact: *95 percent of the material in a spent nuclear fuel rod can be reused.*[253]

NATIONAL PRIORITY

Safety, Security, and Resilience

The authors have championed energy productivity throughout this book. While we note much room for ongoing improvement on this front, the energy and power industries have already begun to embrace efficiency as a worthy goal, especially given future accrual to their bottom line. But history shows that such strides have limited long-term value without precautions against catastrophe.

As the Deepwater Horizon disaster has so painfully underscored, even as a mere business proposition productivity is an inadequate objective if it comes at the expense of less easily measured variables. When companies fail to protect their workers, neighboring communities and the environment, their prosperity—and all of ours—suffers. Estimates for BP's total expected liability for the Gulf spill—including clean-up costs, voluntary compensation and satisfaction of legal claims—had run into the tens of billions by early June, according to the *Wall Street Journal*.[254]

On the other hand, when companies prioritize values like safety, their efforts can bear tremendous fruit. The *New York Times* writes: "The [oil] industry standard for safety, analysts say, is set by ExxonMobil." Not coincidentally, ExxonMobil is the most profitable company (of any kind) in the world.[255]

The future of all major players in the energy space, not least the offshore drilling industry, hinges on striking the right balance between productivity and the values that lead to disaster when neglected: safety, security, and resilience.

Just as safer operations support productivity and profitability, so do more secure operations. In order to protect the nation's critical infrastructure from both unintentional and malicious physical threats, traditional security systems must evolve into better providers of "asset awareness." Once again, they will do so by tapping advanced Information Technology.

But we must go even further than that, because recent history teaches that safety valves and perimeter fences are useful tools but insufficient ones in the face of natural or manmade disasters. Levees break and blowout preventers fail. A robust approach to both safety and security in the energy business goes beyond mere protection. What's required is a more comprehensive organizing principle, known in the all-hazards community as *resilience*.

Chapter 21

Deepwater Drilling

Clean Score	Safety Score	Reliability Score	Affordability Score	X Degree Proven	X Likely Near-term Impact	TOTAL SCORE
20	15	25	25	100%	100%	85

ne of the most notable achievements in the entire energy industry in recent decades is the push by oil & gas operators farther and farther offshore. In 2003, the Discoverer Deep Seas became the first rig to drill in over 10,000 feet of water.[256] Six years later, the Deepwater Horizon drilled to a record total depth of over six miles.[257] That same rig now sits at the bottom of the ocean floor in the Gulf of Mexico.

As M. Elisabeth Paté-Cornell, Chair of the Department of Management Science and Engineering at Stanford University, observes: "In an organization that rewards maximum production, operates most of the time in a rough and generally unforgiving environment, and faces a demanding world market, the culture is marked by formal and informal rewards for pushing the system to the limit of its capacity."[258]

At the limits of capacity, of course, things are more likely to break. The Deepwater Horizon incident is arguably the worst man-made environmental disaster ever seen in the United States.

By late June 2010, BP was throwing $100 million per day at the clean-up effort[259] and had agreed to deposit $20 billion into a claims fund.[260]

Following this accident, everything will change for the offshore oil and gas sector.

The Minerals Management Service, whose coziness with the industry went so far as to include "a culture of substance abuse and promiscuity,"[261] is gone. We now have the Bureau of Ocean Energy Management, Regulation, and Enforcement, which is expected to take a much more hands-on approach to its interaction with operators, perhaps in the manner of the Nuclear Regulatory Commission.

LESSONS LEARNED — AND NOT LEARNED

In the years following the Three Mile Island accident, NRC's response was to introduce a deluge of new regulatory requirements, some of them helpful and some not. On the negative side, the nuclear industry got bogged down in minutiae, and operators found themselves forced to overdesign and overbuild systems to points well beyond levels dictated by sound risk-management practices.

At the same time, positive developments came to the safety culture. We saw a notable shift from deterministic to probabilistic safety assessments,[262] which helped to set priorities rather than to assign every conceivable safety risk equal footing, no matter the impact or likelihood of failure. The industry also broadened its focus to include more human factors, as advanced instrumentation can only prevent so much calamity if inattentive individuals sit at the control panel.

The offshore industry might have learned from Three Mile Island, but that would have required a significant leap of imagination. It's a greater surprise that an accident closer to the industry's bailiwick, the Alpha Piper incident, didn't significantly impact safety procedures for drilling in open water.

The Piper Alpha platform exploded in the U.K. North Sea in 1988, claiming the lives of 167 workers. The post mortem on this event reveals many common threads with the Deepwater Horizon incident, including inadequate redundancies and managers putting productivity over safety.[263]

Now, with another offshore disaster freshly in mind and closer to home, the federal government will react quickly and harshly as it moves to lock down the deepwater drilling business. The recent language about boots on necks and ass kicking makes that clear enough.[264]

The wisest thing for the oil industry to do would be to take a page from the nuclear industry and form its own version of the Institute of Nuclear Power Operations (INPO). The Kemeny Commission's investigation of Three Mile Island recommended that the nuclear industry form a body to promote and share best practices in safety and reliability. That's what INPO does, and it's proven a very effective organization.

As we saw earlier, safer nuclear operations had the additional benefit of leading to improved plant utilization. That development arguably owes less to an overbearing NRC than to the industry's choice to embrace a more stringent safety culture and to take responsibility for oversight of day-to-day plant management. The industry mantra became "anybody's accident is everybody's accident."

If the oil and gas industry can't promulgate a similar cultural shift, there is no future for offshore drilling, and the bureaucrats in Washington won't be the ones to blame. They're just filling a void that shouldn't exist.

Mountains of paperwork lie ahead, and document management for regulatory purposes will become an increasingly important function in the offshore industry. Perhaps solutions the authors have discussed on the nuclear side can be reconfigured to deal with the future challenge of designing, licensing, and building offshore oil and gas infrastructure in a much stricter regulatory environment.

Did You Know: *There are over 27,000 abandoned wells in the Gulf of Mexico.*[265]

Chapter 22

Energy Independence versus Energy Security

Although the two terms often get conflated, "energy security" and "energy independence" are not one and the same. Energy independence is the means to meet all our energy needs without turning to foreign sources. Energy security is the ability to keep the tap flowing, regardless of the source of supply.

Robert Bryce, author of the insightful book *Gusher of Lies*, calls the dream of energy independence "hogwash" and a "dangerous delusion," first because it's not possible and, second, because trying to achieve the impossible distorts markets and wastes resources. He notes, among other things, that for all the handwringing over Persian Gulf oil, it accounted for only 11 percent of all the oil that Americans consumed in 2005.[266] We currently import more oil from Canada than from Saudi Arabia, Iraq, and Kuwait combined.[267] As with any other form of trade or economic activity, our diverse global energy supply lines crisscross the world.

Furthermore, Bryce notes, oil makes up 65 to 95 percent of Persian Gulf exports. "They can't drink it, nor use it to water their palm trees. They must sell it" into a fungible market, he writes.[268] So the Saudis and their neighbors have no realistic incentive for cutting off their supplies to us. And unless they do so completely, their oil—out there in the world market—will likely continue to get factored into the price that we pay.

In any case, with 60 percent of America's crude oil and gasoline needs being met from abroad—and imports constituting nearly all the oil consumed by some European countries—whether we like it or not the world is in a long-term state of energy *inter*dependence.

A more acute issue in the global oil trade is the existence of half a dozen shipping lane chokepoints.[269] This fact speaks not to the challenge of energy independence but to that of energy security.

Dave Forest of Notela Resource Advisors notes that China, for example, receives 80 percent of its oil imports through the Straits of Malacca.[270] It's no wonder that the Chinese increasingly look across the Pacific, at producers like Venezuela and Colombia, in a drive to "escape the Straits."

In terms of fuel supply, global energy security will rest not upon a foundation of autarkic isolationism, but upon an increasingly dense web of interconnections that takes shape through global trade. Rather than wasting resources in pursuit of energy independence for its own sake, national governments would do well to accept the fact of interdependence and focus instead on keeping world supply lines unobstructed.

Think: *Iran sits atop 132 billion barrels of oil reserves yet imports 40 percent of its gasoline.*[271]

Chapter 23

Critical Infrastructure Protection

Clean Score	Safety Score	Reliability Score	Affordability Score	X Degree Proven	X Likely Near-term Impact	TOTAL SCORE
20	25	25	10	100%	80%	64

The greatest challenge to our energy security is the susceptibility of our infrastructure to catastrophic failure. Asset integrity—keeping the nation's refining, generation, transmission, and distribution assets whole and functioning—is a growing challenge.

First of all, the age of our infrastructure makes it vulnerable. Second, our lack of asset awareness, or insight into the status of that infrastructure at any point in time, compounds the vulnerability. Small problems, when left undetected, have a way of snowballing into large problems.

As we saw in Chapter 6, inadequate tree trimming played a role in the Northeast Blackout. Early in 2010, two reactors closed at Calvert Cliffs Nuclear Power Plant in Maryland when melting snow leaked through the roof and caused an electrical fault.[272] Both of these intrusions went undetected until large knock-on effects occurred.

Similarly, the author Lawrence E. Joseph recently noted in a *New York Times* op-ed piece that we are "unready" for inevitable solar storms that can disrupt the grid by causing transformers to melt down. Notes Joseph, without grid-level surge suppressors "a giant pulse can knock out worldwide power systems for months or even years."[273]

The word "security" may conjure images of masked assailants, but our assets are just as likely to be compromised by natural forces as by a hacker or a jihadist. Simple old age is perhaps the single greatest threat to our infrastructure.

NETWORK INTELLIGENCE TO THE RESCUE

In the United States, there are 158,000 miles of high-voltage transmission lines and millions of miles of lower-voltage distribution lines. There are roughly 200,000 miles of oil pipelines and 300,000 miles of pipelines for the gathering and transmission of natural gas.[274] This kind of scale poses formidable obstacles to achieving asset awareness.

The primary tool in pipeline inspection is known as a "pig." When you pig a line, you send an intelligent device through a certain section of the pipe, checking for leaks and other abnormalities. These routine inspections, while valuable, are necessarily infrequent due to cost and time limitations. Why not move to "always-on" sensors that could perform the same monitoring tasks?

A fiber optic cable can monitor pipeline assets for tampering or damage with an acoustic sensitivity that extends for hundreds of miles. Such systems might also limit theft. Though it's less of an issue in the United States, in China oil pilferage is a serious problem. Between 2002 and 2009, Sinopec reportedly encountered around 20,000 incidences of thieves drilling into pipelines.[275]

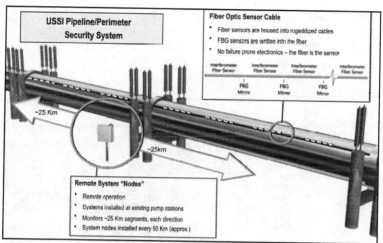

A Single Node of a USSI Pipeline Security System Can Monitor Fifty Kilometers
Source: US Sensor Systems, Inc.

US Sensor Systems, a company that we introduced in Chapter 10, is looking at ways to integrate fiber optics into a host of security solutions, from intrusion detection to structural integrity monitoring.

Another Acorn Energy company, DSIT Solutions, focuses on protection of another security vulnerability: the maritime flank.

As noted in a recent issue of *Jane's Defence Weekly*, "there are billions of dollars worth of facilities and structures under or adjacent to the sea. Governments, and particularly the energy industry, are finally waking up to their vulnerability to attack" by stealthy assailants.[276]

Over 3,000 energy facilities around the world sit near water because of cooling needs or logistical advantages. For example, some nuclear power plants in the U.S. consume over a million gallons of water per minute.[277] Recognizing the threat of a waterborne assailant, the Nuclear Regulatory Commission has mandated that all 104 nuclear power plants install security at their water intake valves.[278]

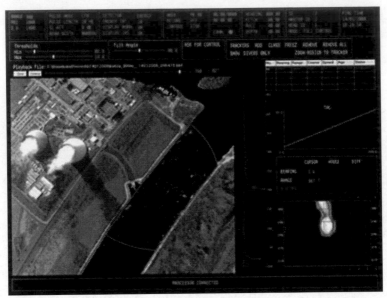

A Underwater Security System Installed at an Energy Facility
Source: DSIT

The maritime equivalent of perimeter monitoring is called multisensory diver-detection sonar (DDS). In relation to the scale of the landscape, a single attacker outfitted with nothing but a breathing apparatus and an explosive device is hard to spot. (Underwater surveillance experts use the term "low-signature target.") Nor is it a simple task to distinguish that diver from a marine mammal.

DSIT stands among the pioneers in this area, having sold around 30 DDS systems all over the world since 2007. The Israeli company believes it has the only solution capable of detecting closed-breather divers at long range with a minimal false-alarm rate.

Saboteur divers might sound like an improbable threat to critical infrastructure, but the Israeli military killed a group of divers reported to be Al Aqsa Martyrs' Brigade members in early June 2010.[279] Iran's Islamic Revolutionary Guard Corps (IRGC) has a video on YouTube purporting to show a squad of divers attacking and destroying an oil infrastructure installation.[280]

CYBERSECURITY

As with our highly interconnected electric grid, the information networks linking energy assets are a dual source of strength and vulnerability. These networks provide us with better real-time information, but that information can also be stolen and abused.

Every once in a while, Americans hear about Chinese or Russian hackers probing our corporate or government networks. Last year, Operation Aurora saw Google and at least 33 other companies targeted by a Chinese cyber attack.[281]

One big fear is of a foreign government-led effort to map our critical infrastructure and deposit software tools that could cripple the nation in the event of a large-scale conflict. Last year the media reported incidences of such power grid hacks, though details were spotty.[282]

It is clear that the energy industry is particularly vulnerable to cyber crime. McAfee has found that attempts at extortion through cyber attacks are most common in the oil & gas and power sectors, where hackers target SCADA (i.e. supervisory control) networks more often than financial data.[283] You don't have to have seen *Live Free or Die Hard* to understand that these infiltrations auger potentially serious consequences. Once again America's Information Technology experts will have to apply great creativity in meeting the threat.

Imagine: There are over 134,000 miles of petroleum pipelines and 387,000 miles of gas pipelines in the U.S. most of which were built before WWII and are now at end of life.[284]

Chapter 24

Resilience

e've taken our share of lumps this decade. If events as diverse as 9/11, Hurricane Katrina, the global financial crisis, and the Deepwater Horizon disaster share a common thread, it's that each involved dealing with the seemingly improbable and each revealed an alarming inability to respond in a timely and concerted fashion when disaster did strike.

Paula Scalingi, president of the Scalingi Group and director of the Pacific Northwest Center for Regional Disaster Resilience, says: "Because protection sooner or later will inevitably fail, the focus must be on cost-effective mitigation measures, damage control, and reconstitution... The [current] focus is on making the nation secure (i.e., keeping bad things from happening) rather than on assuming they may happen and incorporating protection into a comprehensive preparedness approach to dealing with the unthinkable. Such an approach can be defined as resilience."[285]

A comprehensive preparedness approach begins with awareness. Awareness means recognizing that threats exist, taking the initiative to monitor existing conditions for signs of potential threats, and accepting responsibility for dealing with the aftermath. We have the technology to increase situational and asset awareness through sensors, wireless transmitters, and other devices, but this hardware isn't terribly effective without the proper mindset.

Other components of a comprehensive preparedness approach run the gamut from prevention and protection to response and recovery.

The Department of Homeland Security recently adopted ASIS International's Organizational Resilience Standard as part of its Voluntary Private Sector Preparedness (PS-Prep) Program. According to ASIS, the standard "takes an enterprise-wide view of risk management, enabling an organization to develop a comprehensive strategy to prevent when possible, prepare for, mitigate, respond to, and recover from a disruptive incident."[286]

Following the recommendations of the 9/11 Commission, the federal government is taking the concept of resilience seriously. The authors hope to see all companies in the energy and power sectors, so critical to our prosperity and national security, adopt this paradigm as well.

Did You Know: *According to an August 2010* Wall Street Journal *story, a recent report on electric grid security found that: "Many of the security vulnerabilities are strikingly basic and fixable problems, including a failure to install software security patches or poor password management. Many of the fixes would be inexpensive, according to the Idaho National Lab, an Energy Department facility that conducted the study."*[287]

PARTING THOUGHTS

Chapter 25

Knowledge Transmission

E nergy consumption per dollar of GDP has been dropping in the United States for decades:

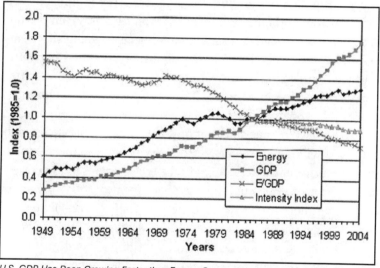

U.S. GDP Has Been Growing Faster than Energy Consumption
Source: U.S. Department of Energy, Energy, Efficiency & Renewable Energy, 2005

Some argue that this phenomenon means that economic growth has decoupled from energy consumption. But the authors believe that conclusion relies too heavily on a narrow conception of energy, one that ignores important qualitative aspects.[288] Rather, we agree with the U.K. Energy Research Centre that "once different energy sources are weighted by their relative 'quality' or economic productivity, the coupling between energy consumption and economic growth appears far stronger."[289]

If we had truly decoupled from energy, no one would need this book. There would be no handwringing about supply shortages or a lack of energy independence. Those concerns linger precisely because our economic outlook remains so tightly coupled to energy consumption.

Humanity's impressive ability to harness ever more useful forms of power has always been one of the keys to rising standards of living. So unless Americans want economic stagnation and falling living standards, the nation must keep investing in energy. But simply building more generation and transmission infrastructure and burning more fuel won't cut it, given the unacceptable safety and environmental impacts of doing so. Greater *productivity* is at least as important as expanded *capacity*. Fortunately, elegant, well-deployed Cleantech innovations offer a higher return on investment than brute-force building does.

In this book, we've touched upon dozens of technologies that we expect to have an equal or greater near-term impact than solar and wind on our energy productivity, environmental footprint, security, and safety. Most of the technologies are so boring to laymen that you'll never hear about them on *60 Minutes* or read about them in *Time* magazine. We can't expect busy consumers to get too fired up about FACTS devices or FE-based reservoir modeling techniques, but we're writing about these things because we're afraid that some remain hidden even to industry participants.

Knowledge, in some ways, is like electric power. When we share it among a network of users, the benefits multiply. But unused, it dissipates. One of the authors' central preoccupations has been the problem of knowledge transmission among participants in an industry filled with information silos. Lots of earnest and smart people work at solving challenges within a particular narrow discipline, without fully appreciating the insights that related enterprises might lend to them.

Having interviewed energy industry experts extensively for this book, we know how much they've got stashed away in the attic. The specialists among them have forgotten more about a given subject than the rest of us will ever know.

If knowledge is power, there's a torrent of power to be unleashed if we could only find a better way to tap the collective experience and expertise of a diverse group of engineers, scientists, entrepreneurs, executives, consultants, investors, and magnificent amateurs.

Everyone actively engaged with the energy and power sectors has an important role to play in the innovation ecosystem. As investors, the authors of this book are in the business of pattern recognition. We draw comparisons across industries, peer around corners, and look for one-foot hurdles to step over.[290] Over a span of 25 years in the trenches of industrial investing, John A. Moore has been a connector, linking entrepreneurs with capital and contacts. Through careful study, independently and on behalf of *The Motley Fool,* Toby Shute has become an energy-industry maven who constantly gathers, filters, and redistributes information.

If you share the mission of making our energy systems cleaner, safer, and more productive, we hope you'll join us in this effort to isolate the best ideas, bring them to the right people, and see that those people get the resources necessary to create value for society.

This is a short book, meant neither to be comprehensive nor definitive. We hope we've shined a light on technologies that have lurked in the shadows, waiting for their turn on stage. We hope, also, that the reader has found in these pages the beginning of a conversation about these remarkable technologies and their chance to help advance the cause of Cleantech.

Of course, the authors have stuck their necks out a little

by rating the various technologies presented here. Perhaps you think we've entirely left out a technology or you disagree with the ratings we assigned. No offense taken. There's wisdom in crowds, especially crowds of the kinds of people we expect to be our most careful readers. We want to hear from you. We are seeking constructive criticism of our thesis and we've started a website to continue the conversation. Go to:

http://www.hiddenCleantech.com

Join us to debate the merits and feasibility of the solutions presented in this book, introduce a technology we missed, share an anecdote, vote your own ratings, or just see what others have to say.

Together we can do more than make and consume energy. We can make energy better.

COMPANIES MENTIONED IN THIS BOOK

ABB (NYSE: ABB)

Acorn Energy (NASDAQ: ACFN)

Alstom (EPA: ALO)

American Electric Power (NYSE: AEP)

Anadarko Petroleum (NYSE: APC)

Apache Corporation (NYSE: APA)

Arch Coal (NYSE: ACI)

Areva (EPA: CEI)

ASIS International

Asplundh Tree Expert Company (private)

Babcock & Wilcox (NYSE: BWC.W)

Baker Hughes (NYSE: BHI)

BC Hydro (Canadian Crown Corporation)

BP (NYSE: BP)

Calera (private)

Cemex (NYSE: CX)

Cenovus Energy (NYSE: CVE)

Chesapeake Energy (NYSE: CHK)

Chevron (NYSE: CVX)

China Huaneng Group

CoaLogix (NASDAQ: ACFN)

Comverge (NASDAQ: COMV)

Coreworx (NASDAQ: ACFN)

Denbury Resources (NYSE: DNR)

Devon Energy (NYSE: DVN)

DSIT Ltd. (NASDAQ: ACFN)

Duke Energy (NYSE: DUK)

Eaton Corporation (NYSE: ETN)

Emerson Electric (NYSE: EMR)

EnCana Natural Gas (NYSE: ECA)

EnerNOC (NASDAQ: ENOC)

EXCEL Services (private)
Exelon (NYSE: EXC)
ExxonMobil (NYSE: XOM)
FirstEnergy (NYSE: FE)
Fluor (NYSE: FLR)
FuelTek (NASDAQ: FTEK)
GE Hitachi Nuclear Energy (joint venture)
General Electric (NYSE: GE)
Grant Prideco (NYSE: NOV)
GridSense (NASDAQ: ACFN)
Halliburton (NYSE: HAL)
Headwaters Incorporated (NYSE: HW)
IBM (NYSE: IBM)
Integrys Energy Group (NYSE: TEG)
Itron (NASDAQ: ITRI)
Joy Mining Machinery (NASDAQ: JOYG)
Landmark Graphics (NYSE: HAL)
Litton Industries (NYSE: NOC)
Massey Energy (NYSE: MEE)
MidAmerican Energy Company (PINK:MDPWK)
Mitchell Energy (NYSE: DVN)
Mitsubishi (TYO:8058)
Nalco Company (NYSE: NLC)
National Oilwell Varco (NYSE: NOV)
Northrop Grumman (NYSE: NOC)
NRG Energy (NYSE: NRG)
Object Reservoir (private)
OpenSpirit (private)
Petrobank (TSE: PBG)
Petroleo Brasileiro (Petrobras) (NYSE: PBR)
PJM Interconnection (private)
QNX Software Systems
Range Resources (NYSE: RRC)
Royal Dutch Shell (NYSE: RDS.A)

Scalingi Group (private)
Schlumberger (NYSE: SLB)
Scottish and Southern Energy (PINK: SSEZY)
Shaw Group (NYSE: SHAW)
Siemens (ETR: SIE)
Sinopec (NYSE: SHI)
Southern Company (NYSE: SO)
Southwestern Energy (NYSE: SWN)
Statoil (NYSE: STO)
Suncor Energy (NYSE: SU)
Telogis (private)
Toshiba (PINK:TOSYY)
Tullow Oil (LON:TLW)
United Technologies (NYSE: UTX)
US Sensor Systems (NASDAQ: ACFN)
Westinghouse (Toshiba and Shaw)
Zilkha Energy

FULL DISCLOSURE

At the time of writing, the authors of this book had financial
interests in the following mentioned companies:

Acorn Energy
GridSense
CoaLogix
Comverge
DSIT
Coreworx
US Sensor Systems

SPECIAL THANKS

This book would not be nearly as polished as it is without the conceptual help and editing of communications coach **Joel E. Fishman**. If you'd like his help, too, please contact him at **scribblertnb@gmail.com**.

ABOUT THE AUTHORS

JOHN A. MOORE has been a director and Chief Executive Officer of Acorn Energy Inc. (ACFN-NASDAQ) since March 2006. He also serves as a director of Voltaix a leading producer of specialty gases used in the production of solar cells and semiconductors. He was previously a Director of Comverge and served on its IPO committee. He serves on the Advisory Council of EnerTech Capital a $350 million energy technology fund. Mr. Moore was formerly President and co-founder of Edson Moore Healthcare Ventures, a fund which acquire $150 million of biotechnology assets from Elan Pharmaceuticals in 2002. John was a cofounder and CEO of Optimer Inc., a specialty materials company that was sold in 2007 to Sterling Capital, a leveraged buyout fund with over $4 Billion under management.

John has invested in many different industries over the past 25 years, but he has never been as excited as he is today about Acorn's opportunities to help create smarter infrastructure. John has four children and one wife. He loves to hear from energy executives, policy wonks and investors. Please contact him at **jmoore@acornenergy.com.**

TOBY SHUTE covers the energy and natural resources sectors for Fool.com, where he has written well over 1,000 articles since becoming a contributor in 2007. He is also an analyst with Motley Fool Special Ops, which focuses on "special situations" investing.

Having majored in Anthropology, Toby has a keen interest in corporate culture, community relations, management/shareholder alignment, and other things that don't show up on a balance sheet. On the number-crunching side, he's working on earning the Chartered Financial Analyst (CFA) designation.

When he's not doing stocks, Toby is hunting for the best in music, food, and film in Brooklyn, where he resides with his wife and dog. He can be reached at **fooltoby@gmail.com.**

ENDNOTES

1   U.S. Census 2007 http://tinyurl.com/2byaaow

2   New York Times article http://tinyurl.com/nyxp28

3   Dan Eggers, Aspen Institute Energy Policy Forum, Credit Suisse Estimate

4   BP Statistical Review of World Energy 2010 http://tinyurl.com/4jaz8p

5   Comverge 2009 10K http://tinyurl.com/2ftktfc

6   http://sites.energetics.com/gridworks/grid.html

7   http://www.api.org/aboutoilgas/

8   U.S. Department of Transportation, Federal Highway Administration, "Highway Statistics 2008, Chart DV1C." Available: http://www.fhwa.dot.gov/policyinformation/statistics/2008/dv1c.cfm

9   Energy Information Administration, "Diesel-A Petroleum Product" http://www.scribd.com/doc/12860647/Encylopedia-of-Energy-Basic

10   U.S. Energy Information Administration, Annual Energy Review 2008, "Consumption by Source and Sector." Available: http://www.eia.doe.gov/emeu/aer/pecss_diagram.html

11   Gregor.us, "The Intractability of the Built Environment." Available: http://gregor.us/alternative-energy/the-intractability-of-the-built-environment/

12   The work of Professor Vaclav Smil was instrumental in clarifying this point for us. We recommend his book *Energy at the Crossroads* (The MIT Press: 2005) as a great place to start investigating his highly accessible scholarship on the subject of energy transitions.

13   A recent study by the National Academies, *Electricity from Renewable Resources: Status, Prospects, and Impediments*, concludes "in the period from 2020 to 2035, it is reasonable to envision that continued and even further accelerated deployment could potentially result in non-hydroelectric renewables providing, collectively, 20 percent or more of domestic electricity generation by 2035." http://www.nap.edu/openbook.php?record_id=12619&page=4

20   Percent penetration within 25 years is within the realm of credibility. 50–100 percent penetration within 10 or 20 years is not.

14   "What we do for a living is really the format of the future because the real answer is going to be getting more out of what you've got." G. Steve Farris quote in the *Wall Street Journal* Tuesday April 20, 2007

15 *McKinsey Quarterly* 2007, Number 1

16 For more on navigating our increasingly networked society, see Kevin Kelly's excellent book *New Rules for the New Economy* (Penguin: 1999), which you can read online at http://www.kk.org/newrules/contents.php

17 See this article by Steve Meloan: http://java.sun.com/developer/technicalArticles/Ecommerce/rfid/

18 Jason Makansi, Lights Out!

19 Huber & Mills, The Bottomless Well

20 http://www.greatachievements.org/

21 U.S.-Canada Power Outage Taskforce, "Final Report on the August 14th Blackout in the United States and Canada." Available: https://reports.energy.gov/

22 Eric Eggers, Credit Suisse, Apen Institute Presentation 2010

23 DOE Smart Grid Report 2009 http://www.oe.energy.gov/DocumentsandMedia/SGSRMain_090707_lowres.pdf

24 For matters of convenience, we are ignoring the carbon required to manufacture the equipment that would make the grid more efficient. Next to the carbon released by generating the amount of energy cited in this paragraph, carbon produced by manufacturing the equipment is negligible.

25 E-Tech Special Report http://www.iec.ch/online_news/etech/arch_2010/etech_0110/special_1.htm

26 ibid

27 http://www.oe.energy.gov/DOE_SG_Book_Single_Pages.pdf

28 Kueck et al 2004

29 http://www.abb.us/cawp/seitp202/1ae34e1fcfe1c99ec12577500066cad5.aspx

30 ibid

31 ibid

32 ibid

33 The Brattle Group, "*Barron's* Cites *Brattle* Report on Electric Utility Infrastructure Investment," January 20, 2008. Available: http://www.brattle.net/NewsEvents/NewsDetail.asp?RecordID=587

34 Announcement: U.S. Department of Energy, "President Obama Announces $3.4 Billion Investments to spur Transition to Smart Energy Grid," October 27, 2009. Available: http://www.energy.gov/news2009/8216.htm

   Breakdown by category: U.S. Department of Energy, "Recovery Act selections for smart grid investment grant awards." Available: http://www.energy.gov/recovery/smartgrid_maps/SGIGSelections_Category.pdf

35 CSC.com, "Study Reveals Opportunity for Global Utilities as Grids Get Smarter," April 12, 2010 . Available: http://www.csc.com/newsroom/press_releases/44249-study_reveals_opportunity_for_global_utilities_as_grids_get_smarter

36 Intelligent Utility, "Consumer Behavior and Electricity Usage," June 16, 2010. Available:
http://www.intelligentutility.com/article/10/06/consumer-behavior-and-electricity-usage

37 Aarp.org, "Smart Meters—Are They Really a Smart Idea?," March 18, 2010:. Available:
http://www.aarp.org/money/budgeting-saving/info-03-2010/smart-meters-are.html

38 Earth2tech,"Smart Meter Backlash, Again: This Time in Texas," March 10, 2010. Available: http://earth2tech.com/2010/03/10/smart-meter-backlash-again-this-time-in-texas/

39 Check out Peter Fox-Penner's book *Smart Power* (Island Press: 2010) for his vision of two future utility business models: the energy service utility and the smart integrator.

40 Here's a *Wall Street Journal* story on decoupling and the resistance it faces: http://online.wsj.com/article/SB123378473766549301.html

Also, check out this paper on when decoupling will and won't work: http://www.ecw.org/ecwresults/kihmdecouplingarticle2009.pdf

41 Newton-Evans 2008

42 American Electric Power, "2010 Corporate Accountability Report." Available: http://www.aepsustainability.com/docs/AEP-AccountabilityReport2010.pdf

43 Better Power Lines Global, "Analysis of Transformer failures, 2003." Available: http://www.bplglobal.net/eng/knowledge-center/download.aspx?id=191

44 http://www.eaton.com/ecm/idcplg?IdcService=GET_FILE&dID=167018

45 PJM,"Smart Grid progresses in PJM region," May 2010. Available: http://pjm.com/~/media/about-pjm/newsroom/2010-releases/20100510-pmu-agreements.ashx

46 For more on synchrophasors and grid reliability, here's an exhaustive report: http://www.naspi.org/news/rapir_final_draft_20100603.pdf

47 Smart Grid Today, "When it comes to homes, how essential is meter part of smart grid?," June 30, 2010,." Available: www.smartgridtoday.com/public/1761print.cfm

48 Energy Central, "PMUs in the Limelight," August 19, 2009. Available: http://www.energycentral.com/gridtandd/gridoperations/articles/2134/PMUs-in-the-Limelight/

49 ABB Inc., "Energy Efficiency in the Power Grid report." Available: http://www04.abb.com/global/seitp/seitp202.nsf/c71c66c1f02e6575c125711f004660e6/64cee320 3250d1b7c12572c8003b2b48/$FILE/Energy+efficiency+in+the+power+grid.pdf

50 GE, "Series Compensation Systems from GE." Available: http://www.gepower.com/prod_serv/products/transformers_vft/en/series_compensation.htm

51 IEEE Power & Energy Society, FACTS Technology Committee, I-4 Working Group

52 For more information, check out this article by Dr. Gregory Reed and his former colleagues at Mitsubishi Electric: http://www.meppi.com/Products/FACTS/Documents/FACTS percent20on percent20Transmission percent20Gridlock.pdf

53 Authors estimate

54 Authors estimate

55 http://en.wikipedia.org/wiki/Utility_pole

56 NERC, "Vegetation related Transmission Outages." Available: http://www.nerc.com//page.php?cid=4|37|257|258

57 http://www.hoovers.com/search/company-search-results/100003765-1.html?type=company&term=asplundh

58 *New Rules for the New Economy* again. Read this book.

59 Electric Energy Online, "Improving Operational Performance Through Automatic Vehicle Management." Available: http://www.electricenergyonline.com/?page=show_article&mag=60&article=455

60 Telogis, "GPS Fleet Management ROI." Available: http://www.telogis.com/benefits/your-roi/

61 http://www.powline.com/vegetation.pdf

62 ibid

63 http://www.electricenergyonline.com/?page=show_article&mag=35&article=274

64 National Energy Technology Laboratory, U.S. Department of Energy, "Energy Storage–A Key Enabler Of The Smart Grid" September 2009. Available: http://www.netl.doe.gov/smartgrid/referenceshelf/whitepapers/Energy percent20Storage_2009_10_02.pdf

65 http://www.solar-reserve.com/technology.html

66 Enel, "At Priolo Enel Inaugurates The "Archimede" Power Plant," July 14, 2010. Available: http://www.enel.com/en-GB/media/press_releases/release.aspx?iddoc=1634858

67 CNN, Bill Gates: "We need global 'energy miracles,'" February 12, 2010. Available: http://www.cnn.com/2010/TECH/02/12/bill.gates.clean.energy/index.html

68 Robert Bryce, Power Hungry page 190

69 U.S. Department of Energy, U.S. Energy Information Administration, Annual Energy Review 2008, U.S. "Primary Energy Consumption by Source and Sector." Available: http://www.eia.doe.gov/emeu/aer/pecss_diagram.html
60.9 quads / 99.2 quads

70 Library of Economics and Liberty, The Concise Encyclopedia of Economics, "Economic Growth." Available: http://www.econlib.org/library/Enc/EconomicGrowth.html

71 Society of Petroleum Engineers, "Frontiers of Technology," February 1999. Available: http://www.spe.org/spe-app/spe/jpt/1999/02/frontiers_seismic.htm

72 ibid

73 Allbusiness.com, "Halliburton Announces Agreement to Acquire Landmark Graphics Corp," July 1, 1996. Available: http://www.allbusiness.com/company-activities-management/company-structures-ownership/7249544-1.html

74 ibid

75 http://www.fossil.energy.gov/programs/oilgas/publications/environ_benefits/12fsexp.pdf

76 U.S. Department of Energy, Office of Fossil Energy, "Environmental Benefits of Advanced Oil and Gas Exploration and Production Technology." Available: http://www.fossil.energy.gov/programs/oilgas/publications/environ_benefits/5explor.pdf

77 OnePetro.org, "Measuring the Impact of 3-D Seismic on Business Performance," June 1999. Available: http://www.onepetro.org/mslib/servlet/onepetropreview?id=00056851&soc=SPE

78 New York Times,"A Wildcatter On the Tame Side; Replacing Roughnecks With Computers," March 20, 1998. Available: http://www.nytimes.com/1998/03/20/business/a-wildcatter-on-the-tame-side-replacing-roughnecks-with-computers.html

79 Tullow Oil, "Exploration Success." Available: http://www.tullowoil.com/index.asp?pageid=48

80 http://www.fossil.energy.gov/programs/oilgas/publications/environ_benefits/12fsexp.pdf

81 American Association of Petroleum Geologists, Explorer October 2002, "Global Depths Have Great Potential." Available: https://aapg.org/explorer/2002/10oct/appex_deepwater.cfm

82 http://www.anadarko.com/About/Pages/Overview.aspx

83 HIS Energy, World Watch, "10-Year Reserve Revisions And Discoveries Outpace Consumption." Available: http://energy.ihs.com/NR/rdonlyres/A80B07BA-B976-4F9B-A319-D490EC768BE1/0/0104worldwatch.pdf

84 http://www.encyclopedia.com/doc/1G1-97994783.html

85 BP, Sir John Browne speech, Sept. 7, 2000, "Forties Field 20th Anniversary." Available: http://www.bp.com/genericarticle.do?categoryId=98&content Id=2000304 and
Apache Corporation, "Forties Import Upgrade transforms field's weakest link," May 2008. Available: http://www.apachecorp.com/explore/Browse_Archives/View_Article.aspx?Article.ItemID=596

86 Apache Corporation, "Forties Field bigger than perceived," December 2005. Available: http://www.apachecorp.com/explore/Browse_Archives/View_Article.aspx?Article.ItemID=335

87 Oil & Gas Journal, "Global Oil Reserves—Recovery Factors Leave Vast Target for EOR Technologies," November 2007. Available: http://www.its.com.ve/publications/Global Oil_ EOR Challenge.pdf

88 Rigzone, "Shell, TU Delft Join Forces in EOR Program," February 10, 2010. Available: http://www.rigzone.com/news/article.asp?a_id=87283

89 Roxar, Turning Information Into Value, January 2008. Available: http://www.roxar.com/getfile.php/Files/Financial percent20Presentations/Corp_pres_2008_DN-BNor2.pdf

90 p. 22, The National Petroleum Council, "Conventional Oil and Gas study," July 18, 2007. Available: http://www.npc.org/Study Topic Papers/19-TTG-Conventional-OG.pdf

91 ibid

92 Digital Energy Journal, "Using Wired Drill Pipes," January 10, 2009. Available: http://www.digitalenergyjournal.com/displaynews.php?NewsID=885& http://www.ioconf.no/2009/presentations/parallel4

93 Rigzone, "Baker Hughes INTEQ Unveils New aXcelerate High-Speed Telemetry Service," November 7,2008. Available: http://www.rigzone.com/news/article.asp?a_id=69095

94 Rigzone, "Baker Hughes INTEQ Unveils New aXcelerate High-Speed Telemetry Service," November 7,2008. Available: http://www.rigzone.com/news/article.asp?a_id=69095

95 U.S. Department of Energy, The National Energy Technology Laboratory, "IntelliPipe™ Technology: Wired for Speed and Durability," June 5, 2003. Available: http://www.netl.doe.gov/publications/press/2003/tl_intellipipe_rmotctest.html

96 Gerson, Lehrman Group, "Seismic While Drilling is Emerging as a Practical Tool to reduce Drilling Costs," August 17, 2009. Available:Seismic While Drilling is Emerging as a Practical Tool to Reduce Drilling CostSeismic While Drilling is Emerging as a Practical Tool to Reduce Drilling Cost http://www.glgroup.com/News/Seismic-While-Drilling-is-Emerging-as-a-Practical-Tool-to-Reduce-Drilling-Cost-42528.html

97 BP Statistical Review of World Energy, 2010

98 http://www.statoil.com/en/OurOperations/ExplorationProd/ncs/statfjord/Statfjord-LateLife/Pages/default.aspx

99 U.S. Department of Energy, The National Energy Technology Laboratory, "Exploration and Production Technologies: Improved Recovery-Enhanced Oil Recovery." Available: http://www.netl.doe.gov/technologies/oil-gas/ep_technologies/improvedrecovery/enhancedoilrecovery/eor.html

100 Denbury Resources Inc., Operations-CO2 EOR." Available: http://www.denbury.com/index.php?id=15

101 ibid and Airgas, "Airgas, Inc. To Acquire Carbonic Industried Corporation And A Major Carbon Dioxide Source/Pipeline," October 29, 1996. Available: http://www.airgas.com/content/pressReleases.aspx?pressrelease_id=884&year=1996

102 Airgas, "Airgas Announces Divestiture of Jackson Dome Carbon Dioxide Reserves and Pipeline," January 18, 2001. Available: http://www.airgas.com/content/pressReleases.aspx?PressRelease_ID=793&year=2001

103 Securities and Exchange Commission, Denbury Resources, 2001 Annual Report to Shareholders. Available: http://www.sec.gov/Archives/edgar/data/945764/000089907802000222/denbury10k2001ex13.txt

104 Securities and Exchange Commission, Denbury Resources, 2008 10-K. Available: http://www.sec.gov/Archives/edgar/data/945764/000095013409004231/d66582e10vk.htm

105 Denbury Resources, "Denbury Resources Announces Record Production Levels; First Quarter 2002 Results." Available: http://phx.corporate-ir.net/phoenix.zhtml?c=72374&p=irol-newsArticle&ID=289620&highlight=

106 Securities and Exchange Commission, Denbury Resources, 2009 10-K. Available: http://www.sec.gov/Archives/edgar/data/945764/000095012310019490/d71173e10vk.htm

107 U.S. Department of Energy, Office of Fossil Energy, National Energy Technology Laboratory, "Oil Exploration & Production Program Enhanced Oil Recovery," June 2005. Available: http://www.netl.doe.gov/technologies/oil-gas/publications/prgmfactsheets/PrgmEOR.pdf

108 GEO ExPro, "breakthrough for repeated seismic," September 2004. Available: http://www.geoexpro.com/sfiles/8/21/6/file/Valhall_26-29.pdf

109 Naval Research Laboratory, Optical Science Division,"Development of the Fiber Optic Wide Aperture Array: From Initial Development to Production," 2004. Available: http://www.nrl.navy.mil/research/nrl-review/2004/optical-sciences/dandridge/

110 Petroleum Geo Services, "Petrobras and PGS Sign Agreement to Perform Fiber-Optic Permanent Seismic Reservoir Monitoring in Brazil's Deepwater Jubarte Field," June 14, 2010. Available: http://www.pgs.com/Pressroom/Press_Releases/Petrobras-and-PGS-Sign-Agreement-to-Perform-Fiber-Optic-Permanent-Seismic-Reservoir-Monitoring-in-Brazils-Deepwater-Jubarte-Field/

111 U.S. Department of Energy, National Energy Technology Laboratory, "Microhole "Designer" Seismic Testing Its Potential in the Field," April 24, 2010. Available: http://www.netl.doe.gov/publications/press/2007/070424-Microhole.html

112 Department of Energy, E&P Focus Volume 1, No.3 3Q 2005

113 Oil & Gas Journal, "Global Oil Reserves—Recovery Factors Leave Vast Target for EOR Technologies," November 2007. Available: http://www.its.com.ve/publications/Global Oil_ EOR Challenge.pdf

114 American Association of Petroleum Geologists, Energy Minerals Division, "Oil Sands." Available: http://emd.aapg.org/technical_areas/oil_sands.cfm

115 The Pembina Institute, Driller Deeper, March 2010. Available: http://pubs.pembina.org/reports/in-situ-report-card-factsheet.pdf

116 Wall Street Journal, "Canadian Oil Production To Grow 60% By 2025 - Industry Group ", June 9, 2010. Available: http://online.wsj.com/article/BT-CO-20100609-714115.html?mod=WSJ_latestheadlines

117 U.S. Department of Energy, Energy Information Administration, "Canada Energy Data, Statistics and Analysis-Oil, Gas, Electricity and Coal," July 2009. Available: http://www.eia.doe.gov/cabs/canada/Oil.html

118 http://geology.com/research/barnett-shale-father.shtml

119 http://geology.com/research/barnett-shale-father.shtml

120 http://www.propublica.org/special/hydraulic-fracturing-national

121 Society of Petroleum Engineers, Frontiers of Technology, July 1999. Available: http://www.spe.org/spe-app/spe/jpt/1999/07/frontiers_horiz_multilateral.htm

122 ibid

123 PR Newswire, "Devon Energy to Acquire Mitchell Energy for $3.5 Billion," August 14, 2001. Available: http://www2.prnewswire.com/cgi-bin/stories.pl?ACCT=104&STORY=/www/story/08-14-2001/0001554164&EDATE

124 Republic Energy, Energy, "The Barnett Shale: not so simple after all." Available: http://www.republicenergy.com/Articles/Barnett_Shale/Barnett.aspx

125 Devon Energy, "Devon Barnett Shale Q&A," May 20, 2010. Available: http://www.devonenergy.com/ir/Documents/052010 percent20- percent20DVN percent-20Barnett percent20QA.pdf

126 http://www.swn.com/aboutswn/Pages/ourhistory.aspx

127 For The Motley Fool's past coverage of this phenomenon, see: http://www.fool.com/investing/dividends-income/2009/10/20/the-amazing-shale-race.aspx and http://www.fool.com/investing/international/2009/11/27/a-global-shale-gas-update.aspx

128 Massachussets Institute of Technology, "The Future of Natural Gas," 2010. Available: http://web.mit.edu/mitei/research/studies/report-natural-gas.pdf

129 http://www.glossary.oilfield.slb.com/display.cfm?term=wet percent20gas

130 Potential Gas Committee, "Potential Gas Committee Reports Unprecedented Increase in Magnitude of U.S. Natural Gas Resource Base" June 18, 2009

131 http://www.intel.com/technology/mooreslaw/

132 Inmotiononline, "Oil experts probe 'field of the future' technology," June 19, 2007. Available: http://www.inmotiononline.com.au/news/6135-Oil-experts-probe-field-of-the-future-technology

133 http://www.energy-cg.com/wsjdigitaloilfieldarticle.html

134 Society of Petroleum Engineers, "Reducing the "Data Commute" Heightens E&P Productivity," JPT, September 2009. Available: http://www.spe.org/jpt/print/archives/2009/09/13Management.pdf

135 http://www.energistics.org/

136 Oilit, "SPE Digital Energy," 2007. Available: http://www.oilit.com/1_tw/2007_contents/0705_SPEDigitalEnergy_contents.pdf

137 Hydrocarbon Processing, "Improving Refinery Reliability , Performance and Utilization," October 2007. Available: http://www2.emersonprocess.com/siteadmincenter/PM percent20Articles/hycbproc0710_motiva.pdf

138 Emerson Process Management, "Emerson's Smart Wireless solutions enable temperature profiling and tank level measurement redundancy at PPG," September 10, 2007. Available: http://www.emersonprocess.com/home/news/pr/709_ppg.html

139 Energy Information Administration http://www.eia.doe.gov/pub/oil_gas/petroleum/analysis_publications/oil_market_basics/demand_text.htm

140 U.S. Department of Energy, U.S. Energy Information Administration, Annual Energy Review, "U.S. Primary Energy Consumption by Source and Sector, 2008." Available: http://www.eia.doe.gov/emeu/aer/pecss_diagram.html

141 ibid

142 http://www.archcoal.com/aboutus/BT percent20Brochure.pdf

143 http://www.sandiegozoo.org/animalbytes/t-elephant.html

144 From 0.76 in 1950 to 5.99 in 2008: http://www.eia.doe.gov/emeu/aer/txt/ptb0706.html

145 United States Department of Labor, Mine Safety and Health Administration, "Coal Fatalities for 1900 Through 2009." Available: http://www.msha.gov/stats/centurystats/coalstats.asp

146 http://www.joy.com/Joy/Products/Longwall-Systems/Longwall-Shearers.htm

147 http://www.mining-technology.com/projects/twentymile/

148 Popular Mechanics, "High-Tech Mining Makes Coal King of Fossil Fuels, But Is It Clean?," October 1, 2009. Available: http://www.popularmechanics.com/science/environment/4219178

149 CoalAge, "America's Most Productive Underground Mines Hold Steady," February 18, 2010. Available: http://www.coalage.com/index.php/features/212-americas-most-productive-underground-mines-hold-steady.html

150 The Charleston Gazette, "Four years after Sago, few mines have new communications gear," March 20, 2010. Available: http://wvgazette.com/News/BeyondSago/201003200362

151 U.S. Department of Energy, U.S. Energy Information Administration, "Coal Production and Number of Mines by State and Mine Type," September 18, 2009. Available: http://www.eia.doe.gov/cneaf/coal/page/acr/table1.html

152 http://www.archcoal.com/aboutus/BT percent20Brochure.pdf

153 http://www.qnx.com/company/customer_stories/ss_170_2.html

154 U.S. Geological Survey http://energy.usgs.gov/factsheets/coalavailability/coal.html

155 International Energy Agency, "The Economics of Transition in the Power Sector," January 2010. Available: http://www.iea.org/papers/2010/economics_of_transition.pdf

156 ibid

157 ibid

158 EU: http://online.wsj.com/article/BT-CO-20100618-706544.html
Canada: Power-Gen Worldwide, "Coal-fired power plants to be phased out in Canada," June 23, 2010. Available: http://www.powergenworldwide.com/index/display/articledisplay/0550767736/articles/powergenworldwide/coal-generation/o-and-m/2010/06/Canada-coal-phase-out.html

159 http://www.babcock.com/products/boilers/up_specs.html

160 http://www.babcock.com/products/boilers/supercritical.html

161 Power magazine, "MidAmerican's Walter Scott, Jr. Energy Center Unit 4 earns POWER's highest honor," August 15, 2007. Available: http://www.powermag.com/coal/MidAmericans-Walter-Scott-Jr-Energy-Center-Unit-4-earns-POWERs-highest-honor_210.html

162 https://www.swepco.com/global/utilities/lib/docs/info/projects/TurkPlant/supercriticalfactsheet.pdf

163 Specs on Yuhuan: http://www.power-technology.com/projects/yuhuancoal/
We should note that plant efficiency is not well defined or uniformly reported. See this article from *POWER* Magazine: http://www.powermag.com/coal/Plant-Efficiency-Begin-with-the-Right-Definitions_2432.html

164 The National Coal Council says 35 percent: http://www.nationalcoalcouncil.org/Documents/Advanced_Coal_Technologies.pdf

165 Reuters, "Southern Co unit to build Mississippi coal plant," May 27, 2010. Available: http://www.reuters.com/article/idUSN2726108120100528?type=marketsNews

166 Securities and Exchange Commission, "Summary of Edwardsport IGCC Project," April 16, 2010. Available: http://www.sec.gov/Archives/edgar/data/81020/000110465910020041/a10-7658_1ex99d1.htm

167 Reuters, "Mitsubishi plans next-gen coal power in China—Nikkei," June 3, 2010. Available: http://www.reuters.com/article/idUSSGE6520I820100603?type=marketsNews

168 The Huffington Post, "China's Going Supercritical—A Critical Test For China And World?," June 9, 2010. Available: http://www.huffingtonpost.com/bill-chameides/chinas-going-supercritica_b_605731.html

169 Trend from 1970: http://www.epa.gov/airtrends/images/comparison70.jpg
Trend from 1980: http://www.epa.gov/airtrends/aqtrends.html
Trend from 1990: see page 7, http://www.epa.gov/airtrends/2010/report/fullreport.pdf

170 United States Environmental Protection Agency, "EPA Sets Stronger National Air Quality Standard for Sulfur Dioxide First new SO2 standard in 40 years will improve air quality for millions," June 3, 2010. Available: http://yosemite.epa.gov/opa/admpress.nsf/6424ac1caa800aab85257359003f5337/f137260029b9b4f385257737004e521b!OpenDocument

171 Michigan Department of Natural Resources and Environment, "Mercury Emission Rules Finalized," October 19, 2009. Available: http://www.michigan.gov/deq/0,1607,7-135--224487--,00.html

172 http://www.integrysgroup.com/environment/weston.aspx

173 http://www.duke-energy.com/about-us/cliffside-overview.asp and http://www.duke-energy.com/about-us/cliffside-air-quality.asp

174 http://www.epa.gov/ttn/chief/trends/trends02/pm25_pm10_fil_eguonly_03302009.xls

175 http://www.iea-coal.org.uk/site/ieacoal_old/clean-coal-technologies-pages/wet-scrubbers-for-so2-control?

176 U.S. Department of Energy, U.S. Energy Information Administration, Electric Power Annual, "Number and Capacity of Fossil-Fuel Steam-Electric Generators with Environmental Equipment," 1997 through 2008. Available: http://www.eia.doe.gov/cneaf/electricity/epa/epat3p10.html

Coal nameplate capacity: 337,300 MW http://www.eia.doe.gov/cneaf/electricity/epa/epat1p2.html

177 U.S. Department of Energy, U.S. Energy Information Administration, Electric Power Annual, "Electric Power Industry 2008: Year in Review." Available: http://www.eia.doe.gov/cneaf/electricity/epa/epa_sum.html

178 http://www.lawrencepumps.com/products/rowa_mc.html

179 Power magazine, "Update: What's That Scrubber Going to Cost?," March 1, 2009. Available: http://www.powermag.com/business/Update-Whats-That-Scrubber-Going-to-Cost_1743.html

180 U.S. Environmental Protection Agency, "Coal-Fired Power Plant Heat Rate Reductions," January 22, 2009. Available: http://www.epa.gov/airmarkt/resource/docs/coalfired.pdf

181 Power magazine, "MidAmerican's Walter Scott, Jr. Energy Center Unit 4 earns POWER's highest honor," August 15, 2007. Available: http://www.powermag.com/coal/MidAmericans-Walter-Scott-Jr-Energy-Center-Unit-4-earns-POWERs-highest-honor_210_p4.html

182 http://www.iea-coal.org.uk/site/ieacoal_old/clean-coal-technologies-pages/low-nox-burners

183 http://www.iea-coal.org.uk/site/ieacoal_old/clean-coal-technologies-pages/selective-catalytic-reduction-scr-for-nox-control

184 U.S. Department of Energy, National Energy Technology Laboratory, "Clean Coal Technology Report," July 1997. Available: http://www.netl.doe.gov/technologies/coalpower/cctc/topicalreports/pdfs/topical9.pdf

185 http://portfolio.epri.com/ProgramTab.aspx?sId=GEN&rId=166&pId=5558

186 Table 8.8: http://www.eia.doe.gov/oiaf/aeo/assumption/pdf/electricity_tbls.pdf

187 http://www.coalogix.com/news-releases/102-coalogix-reaction-to-the-recent-cair-decision

188 Some background on mercury controls from the GAO: http://www.gao.gov/new.items/d05612.pdf

And from the DOE:

http://www.netl.doe.gov/technologies/coalpower/ewr/pubs/mercuryR&D-v4-0505.pdf

189 Electric Power Research Institute, EPRI Journal, Spring 2010. Available: http://mydocs.epri.com/docs/CorporateDocuments/EPRI_Journal/2010-Spring/1020933_Development.pdf

190 U.S. Department of Energy, National Energy Technology Laboratory, "NETL Technologies Earn Prestigious R&D 100 Awards," July 23, 2009. Available:http://www.netl.doe.gov/publications/press/2009/09048-NETLTechnologies_Earn_Prestigious.html

191 http://www.netl.doe.gov/publications/proceedings/07/mercury/panels/Rini_Panel.pdf

192 McIlvaine Study http://home.mcilvainecompany.com/

193 U.S. Department of Energy, U.S. Energy Information Administration, "Carbon Dioxide Uncontrolled Emission Factors," data for 2008. Available: http://www.eia.doe.gov/cneaf/electricity/epa/epata3.html

194 U.S. Department of Energy, U.S. Energy Information Administration, "Emissions of Greenhouse Gases Report," December 3, 2009. Available: http://www.eia.doe.gov/oiaf/1605/ggrpt/carbon.html

195 U.S. Environmental Protection Agency, "Endangerment and Cause or Contribute Findings for Greenhouse Gases under Section 202(a) of the Clean Air Act," July 2010. Available: http://www.epa.gov/climatechange/endangerment.html

196 ftp://ftp.cmdl.noaa.gov/ccg/co2/trends/co2_mm_mlo.txt

197 Worldchanging.com, "350 ppm," January 2, 2008. Available: http://www.world-changing.com/archives/007744.html

198 http://my.barackobama.com/page/content/newenergy_campaign

199 For a thorough treatment of the subject, see MIT's *The Future of Coal* study: http://web.mit.edu/coal/The_Future_of_Coal.pdf

200 Advance Resources International, "Beyong Wedges: Achieving the Obama Administration's Goals for Reducing Greenhouse Gas Emissions," May 1, 2009. Available:
http://www.adv-res.com/pdf/ARI percent20Beyond percent20Wedges percent205_1_09.pdf

201 U.S. Department of Energy, U.S. Energy Information Administration, Electric Power Annual 2008, "Existing Net Summer Capacity by Energy Source and Producer Type." Available: http://www.eia.doe.gov/cneaf/electricity/epa/epat1p1.html

202 U.S. Department of Energy, U.S. Energy Information Administration, Electric Power Annual 2008, "U.S. Electric Industry Generating Capacity by State." Available: http://www.eia.doe.gov/cneaf/electricity/epa/fig1p1.html

203 http://sequestration.mit.edu/tools/projects/sse_ferrybridge.html

204 Table A-3.E.3, http://web.mit.edu/coal/The_Future_of_Coal.pdf

205 The Carbon Mitigation Association, Scientific American, "Can We Bury Global Warming?," 2005. Available: http://cmi.princeton.edu/resources/pdfs/bury_global-warming.pdf

206 U.S. Department of Energy, U.S. Energy Information Administration, "State Ranking 2. Crude Oil Production, March 2010." Aavailable: http://www.eia.doe.gov/state/state_energy_rankings.cfm?keyid=28&orderid=1

207 Tables EX-2 and 2, http://www.adv-res.com/pdf/ARI percent20Beyond percent-20Wedges percent205_1_09.pdf

208 http://www.statoil.com/en/TechnologyInnovation/ProtectingTheEnvironment/CarboncaptureAndStorage/Pages/CarbonDioxideInjectionSleipnerVest.aspx

209 http://www.calera.com/index.php/technology/technology_vision/

210 International Energy Agency, "CO2 Emissions from Fuel Combustion 2009 http://www.iea.org/co2highlights/co2highlights.pdf

211 World Nuclear Association, "Nuclear Power in France," August 2010. Available: http://www.world-nuclear.org/info/inf40.html

212 U.S. Department of Energy, U.S. Energy Information Administration, Electric Power Annual 2008, "U.S. Electric Power Industry Net Generation." Available: http://www.eia.doe.gov/cneaf/electricity/epa/figes1.html

213 U.S. Department of Energy, U.S. Energy Information Administration, "International Energy Statistics." Available: http://tonto.eia.doe.gov/cfapps/ipdbproject/iedindex3.cfm?tid=2&pid=27&aid=12&cid=&syid=2004&eyid=2008&unit=BKWH

214 The Wall Street Journal,"America's New Nuclear Option," March 23, 2010. Available: http://online.wsj.com/article/SB1000142405274870423130457509213023999278.html

215 Bloomberg Businessweek, "Southern Co. setting stage to build new reactors," June 18, 2010. Available: http://www.businessweek.com/ap/financialnews/D9G-DURKOO.htm

216 The New York Times, "Vermont Senate Votes to Close Nuclear Plant," February 24, 2010. Available: http://www.nytimes.com/2010/02/25/us/25nuke.html

217 Cnet news, "Newsmaker: From Ecowarrior To Nuclear Champion," January 31, 2008. Available: http://news.cnet.com/From-ecowarrior-to-nuclear-champion/2008-13840_3-6228461.html

218 This is a go-to study for anyone desiring to dig deeper into the issues we touch on in this book. At 650 pages, it's perhaps the most comprehensive report out there: http://books.nap.edu/openbook.php?record_id=12091&page=477

219 U.S. Department of Energy, U.S. Energy Information Administration, "Nuclear Generating Units, 1955-2009." Available: http://www.eia.doe.gov/emeu/aer/txt/ptb0901.html

220 International Atomic Energy Agency, "50 years of Energy." Available: http://www.iaea.org/About/Policy/GC/GC48/Documents/gc48inf-4_ftn3.pdf

221 U.S. Department of Energy, U.S. Energy Information Administration, "Nuclear Generating Units, 1955-2009." Available: http://www.eia.doe.gov/emeu/aer/txt/ptb0901.html

222 U.S. Department of Energy, U.S. Energy Information Administration, "Nuclear Power Plant Operations, 1957-2009." Available: http://www.eia.doe.gov/emeu/aer/txt/ptb0902.html

223 ibid

224 http://www.eia.doe.gov/cneaf/nuclear/page/analysis/nuclearpower.html
More on the nuclear fuel cycle here: http://www.world-nuclear.org/info/inf03.html

225 United States Nuclear Regulatory Commission, "Power Uprates for Nuclear Plants," February 2008. Available: http://www.nrc.gov/reading-rm/doc-collections/fact-sheets/power-uprates.html

226 United States Nuclear Regulatory Commission, "Power Uprates for Nuclear Plants," February 2008. Available: http://www.nrc.gov/reading-rm/doc-collections/fact-sheets/power-uprates.html

227 Seeking Alpha, "The Shaw Group Inc F1Q10 (Qtr End 11/30/09) Earnings Call Transcript," January 6, 2010. Available: http://seekingalpha.com/article/181288-the-shaw-group-inc-f1q10-qtr-end-11-30-09-earnings-call-transcript?part=qanda

228 ibid

229 http://www.exeloncorp.com/performance/growthstrategy/Pages/overview.aspx

230 More on EXCEL at their website: http://www.excelservices.com/

231 http://www.nrc.gov/reactors/operating/licensing/techspecs.html

232 Estimate by EXCEL Services

233 Government Computer News, "Scientists creating advanced computer simulation of nuclear reactor," January 2, 2010. Available: http://gcn.com/articles/2010/06/02/virtual-reactor.aspx

234 Sandia National Laboratories, "Sandia to play major role in DOE-funded simulation of "virtual" nuclear reactor," June 14, 2010. Available: https://share.sandia.gov/news/resources/news_releases/virtual_reactor/

235 International Atomic Energy Agency, Bulletin 50-1, September 2008. Available: http://www.iaea.org/Publications/Magazines/Bulletin/Bull501/50104722831.pdf

236 For more info on third generation reactors: http://www.world-nuclear.org/info/inf08.html

237 Bloomsberg Businessweek, " Areva's Overruns at Finnish Nuclear Plant Approach Initial Cost," June 24, 2010. Available: http://www.businessweek.com/news/2010-06-24/areva-s-overruns-at-finnish-nuclear-plant-approach-initial-cost.html

238 http://www.stpnoc.com/FYI.htm

239 Coreworx, "Babcock & Wilcox Selects Coreworx Support Software for its B&W mPower™ Nuclear Reactor," December 29, 2009. Available: http://www.coreworxinc.com/content/news/babcock-wilcox-selects-coreworx-support-software-its-bw-mpower™-nuclear-reactor

240 *Nuclear Implosions* by Daniel Pope, page 126. Available on Google books: http://books.google.com/books?id=6OWFheGYDpoC&lpg=PA125&ots=Jzv7F0wjU4&dq= percent22management percent20study percent20of percent20the percent20roles percent20and percent20relationships percent22&pg=PA125#v=onepage&q&f=false

241 Fluor, "Fluor Awarded Contract to Support Planned New Nuclear Plants at South Texas Project," August 16, 2007. Available: http://investor.fluor.com/phoenix.zhtml?c=124955&p=irol-newsArticle&ID=1041170&highlight

242 Coreworx, "Coreworx' ITAAC Solution for Nuclear delivers quickest path to NRC compliance, ITAAC closure and fuel load," June 23, 2010. Available: http://www.coreworxinc.com/content/news/coreworx-itaac-solution-nuclear-delivers-quickest-path-nrc-compliance-itaac-closure-and

243 Here's a presentation on the licensing process for a new nuclear plant: http://www.ne.doe.gov/energypolicyact2005/Workshop/Jerry% percent20Wilson% percent20Presentation.pdf

244 http://www.nrc.gov/public-involve/conference-symposia/ric/past/2010/slides/th29bellrhv.pdf

245 Energy Information Administration, "Federal Financial Interventions and Subsidies in Energy Markets in 2007," April 2008

246 http://online.wsj.com/article/SB100014240527487042313045750921302399992728.html

247 http://www.nrc.gov/reactors/advanced/4s.html

248 http://www.nrc.gov/reactors/advanced/prism.html

249 http://www.babcock.com/products/modular_nuclear/

250 Roanoke.com, "Babcock & Wilcox: New nukes?," June 6, 2010. Available: http://www.roanoke.com/business/wb/249225

251 http://publicutilities.utah.gov/news/waveofusplantretirementslikelyapproaching.pdf

252 Nuclear Engineering International, "B&W's baby," November 13, 2009. Available: http://www.neimagazine.com/story.asp?storyCode=2054744

253 http://www.world-nuclear.org/info/inf69.html

254 The Wall Street Journal, "BP Oil Spill Cost: $20 Billion? Try $63 Billion," June 16, 2010. Available: http://blogs.wsj.com/marketbeat/2010/06/18/bp-oil-spill-brief-history-of-the-incredible-rising-cost-estimate/

255 Billshrink.com, "The World's Most Profitable Companies," December 21, 2009. Available: http://www.billshrink.com/blog/6715/the-worlds-most-profitable-companies/
Readers may note that BP comes in at Number 5 in this 2008 list. Total liability for *Deep Water Horizon*, however, will likely wipe out two times that year's profit. Readers may also be interested to see our friend and colleague Joe Magyer's take on ExxonMobil at: http://www.fool.com/investing/dividends-income/2009/04/08/the-greatest-company-in-the-history-of-the-world.aspx

256 Transocean, "Transocean Inc. and ChevronTexaco Announce New World Water-Depth Drilling Record in 10,011 Feet of Water," November 17, 2003. Available: http://www.deepwater.com/fw/main/Transocean-Inc-and-ChevronTexaco-Announce-New-World-Water-Depth-Drilling-Record-in-10-011-Feet-of-Water-20C4.html

257 http://www.deepwater.com/fw/main/IDeepwater-Horizon-i-Drills-Worlds-Deepest-Oil-and-Gas-Well-419C151.html

258 Risk Analysis, "Learning from the Piper Alpha Accident: A Postmortem Analysis of Technical and Organizational Factors," Vol. 13, No. 2, 1993. Available: http://www.stanford.edu/group/mse278/cgi-bin/wordpress/wp-content/uploads/2010/01/Learning-from-Piper-Alpha.pdf

259 The Wall Street Journal, " BP's Spending on Gulf Oil Spill Hits $100 Million A Day," June 28, 2010. Available: http://blogs.wsj.com/source/2010/06/28/bps-spending-on-gulf-oil-spill-hits-100-million-a-day/

260 BP, "BP Establishes $20 Billion Claim Fund For Deepwater Horizon Spill And Outlines Dividend Decisions," June 16, 2010. Available: http://www.bp.com/genericarticle.do?categoryId=2012968&contentId=7062966

261 The Washington Post, "Report Says Oil Agency Ran Amok," September11, 2008. Available: http://www.washingtonpost.com/wp-dyn/content/article/2008/09/10/AR2008091001829.html

262 http://www.nuce.boun.edu.tr/psaover.html

263 This should be required reading at the Bureau of Ocean Energy: http://www.stanford.edu/group/mse278/cgi-bin/wordpress/wp-content/uploads/2010/01/Learning-from-Piper-Alpha.pdf

264 Interior Secretary Ken Salazar: "We will keep our boot on their neck until the job gets done." http://www.reuters.com/article/idUSTRE6430AR20100524
President Obama: "We talk to these folks because they potentially have the best answers, so I know whose ass to kick." http://www.cnn.com/2010/POLITICS/06/07/gulf.oil.obama/index.html

265 Msnbc.com, "Gulf awash in 27,000 abandoned wells," July 7, 2010. Available: http://www.msnbc.msn.com/id/38113914/ns/disaster_in_the_gulf/

266 *Gusher of Lies: The Dangerous Delusions of "Energy Independence"* by Robert Bryce (PublicAffairs: 2008)

267 YTD imports through April: Canada, 1,921 thousand barrels per day Saudi Arabia, Iraq, and Kuwait combined: 1,759 thousand barrels per day http://www.eia.doe.gov/pub/oil_gas/petroleum/data_publications/company_level_imports/current/import.html

268 Ibid.

269 http://www.eia.doe.gov/cabs/World_Oil_Transit_Chokepoints/Background.html

270 Pierce Points, "Get the $%#^! Out of Malacca," June 21, 2010. Available: http://www.piercepoints.com/print_letter.php?newsletter=2010_06_21_Pierce_Points.html

271 Reuters Africa, "Iran fuel imports nosedive as sanctions bite-source," July 26, 2010. Available: http://af.reuters.com/article/energyOilNews/idAFLDE66P-1GA20100726

272 The Baltimore Sun, "Calvert Cliffs shutdown probed," February 24, 2010. Available: http://articles.baltimoresun.com/2010-02-24/business/bal-bz.gr.nuke-24feb24_1_calvert-cliffs-nrc-reactor

273 "The Sun Also Surprises" by Lawrence E. Joseph, *New York Times,* August 15, 2010.

274 Department of Homeland Security, "National Infrastructure Protection Plan-Energy Sector." Available: http://www.dhs.gov/xlibrary/assets/nipp_energy.pdf

275 Energy Tribune, "Leaking from China's Oil and Gas Pipelines," June 9, 2010. Available: http://www.energytribune.com/articles.cfm/4303/Leaking-from-Chinas-Oil-and-Gas-Pipelines

276 Jane's Defence Weekly, "Taking Guard: Diver Detection Sonars," June 1, 2010. Available: http://www.acornenergy.com/rsc/articles/news-189.pdf

277 Union of Concerned Scientists, "Got Water?," December 4, 2007. Available: http://www.ucsusa.org/assets/documents/nuclear_power/20071204-ucs-brief-got-water.pdf

278 Safeguards Technology LLC, Nuclear Site Security Update, "Water Intake Security Regulations," November 30, 2010. Available: http://www.safeguards.com/ecommerce/NuclearSiteSecurity12-2009.html

279 The Washington Post, "At least four Palestinian divers shot, killed off Gaza by Israeli navy," June 8, 2010. Available: http://www.washingtonpost.com/wp-dyn/content/article/2010/06/07/AR2010060700825.html

280 http://www.youtube.com/watch?v=zOPDVHM_07o

281 Wired, "Google Hack Attack Was Ultra Sophisticated, New Details Show," January 14, 2010. Available: http://www.wired.com/threatlevel/2010/01/operation-aurora/

282 Greenbiz.com, "Was the Chinese-Russian Power Grid Hack a Hoax?," April 13, 2009. Available: http://www.greenbiz.com/blog/2009/04/13/was-chinese-russian-power-grid-hack-hoax

283 http://newsroom.mcafee.com/images/10039/In percent20the percent20Crossfire_CIP percent20report.pdf

284 Environmental Research Consulting, "Analysis Of Oil Spill Trends In The United States And Worldwide." Available: http://www.environmental-research.com/publications/pdf/spill_statistics/paper4.pdf

285 The Center for Infrastructure Protection at George Mason University has a wonderful collection of materials on this subject. This paper by Paula Scalingi has most strongly shaped our views on the resilience framework (see pp. 55-77): http://cip.gmu.edu/archive/CIPP_Resilience_Series_Monograph.pdf

286 Asis International, "ASIS International Organizational Resilience ANSI Standard Officially Adopted by Department of Homeland Security," June 15, 2010. Available: http://www.asisonline.org/newsroom/pressReleases/2010-06-15_PSprep.doc

287 The Wall Street Journal, "Grid Is Vulnerable to Cyber-Attacks," August 3, 2010. Available: http://online.wsj.com/article/NA_WSJ_PUB: SB10001424052748704905004575405741051458382.html

288 These nuances are discussed in Peter Huber and Mark Mills' *The Bottomless Well* (Basic Books: 2006), which sits near the top of our recommended reading list.

289 http://www.ukerc.ac.uk/Downloads/PDF/07/0710ReboundEffect/0710ReboundEffectReport.pdf

290 The hurdle-stepping notion is Buffett's: http://www.fool.com/investing/value/2010/02/22/buffetts-words-of-wisdom.aspx